Interviewing

and

Interrogation

for Law Enforcement

WITHDRAWN

John E. Hess

anderson publishing co.
2035 Reading Rd.
Cincinnati, OH 45202
1-800-582-7295

Interviewing and Interrogation for Law Enforcement

ISBN 0-87084-348-6
Library of Congress Catalog Number 97-73251

EDITOR Elisabeth Roszmann Ebben
ASSISTANT EDITOR Elizabeth A. Shipp
ACQUISITIONS EDITOR Michael C. Braswell

Dedication

To my wife, Jean, for her faith and patience, and
with thanks to Pat, Sue, Margo, Steve, and Ursula.

Acknowledgments

Nearly one-quarter of a century of wrestling with the problem of obtaining information from other people, often with little or no success, has caused me to reach out to many sources for help. Most of what I know about the topic I learned from these sources, but often I am unable to pinpoint exactly where, when, or how I acquired this knowledge. However, I suspect that much of it came from multiple sources through the years, and has melded into one eclectic philosophy.

Although nearly 15 years as a field agent contributed to my knowledge of interviews and interrogations, much of what I learned came from other sources, including the publications listed at the end of each chapter. While a few of them might qualify as references, most represent a sampling of the material that has influenced my philosophy of this topic and primarily are provided for the reader who desires more detailed coverage of the material.

However, information obtained from all the publications pales when compared with the insight and knowledge provided by the many practitioners, a few of whom are named below, that I have encountered. Warren Holmes in his presentations at the FBI Academy showed that interrogators can also be teachers. His years of experience as a polygrapher and interrogator give him credibility that few others have. Joseph Buckley and other members of John E. Reid and Associates, through their training programs throughout the country, have done much to advance the level of interviewing and interrogation in both the public and private sector. Joseph Kulis, a psychologist who has worked with the Chicago Police Department for many years, has managed to bridge the gap between the clinician and the police officer. He provides practical advice for dealing with human nature. James Earle, Joseph Kenney, and Ron Hilley, all FBI agents, all polygraphers, and most important, all teachers, have provided more knowledge and insight than I can ever calculate.

Finally, I must give credit to the thousands of students, rookie and veteran, local and international, who have shared their experiences with me over the years. I would have needed several lifetimes to gain firsthand all the knowledge that these students and the other sources have provided.

Table of Contents

Prologue

"Hey Joe, got your yearly letter from that creep, I see," growled Al as he sorted through the stack of incoming papers in their mutual mail box. Joe and Al had been assigned to the homicide squad for over twelve years, and although their methods differed, each had put his share of killers in jail during that time.

Joe glanced at the letter Al had tossed to him, opened it and began reading:

October 14

Dear Joe,

It's been just over five years now, and I just wanted to let you know I still haven't forgotten what you did for me. If it hadn't been for you . . .

"You know, Joe," interrupted Al, "I'll never figure that one out. We had nothing on that guy. There wasn't a shred of evidence that he had killed that girl. God knows I tried to find some; I beat the bushes for months for nothing—no witnesses, no forensics, nothing. He knew it too because when I realized we had nothing to lose, I took a shot. I tried to convince him that we had enough to hang him. He just laughed and told me to go ahead and try it.

"Then you come along and shoot the breeze with him, and he spills his guts even though you didn't have a damn thing to offer him. If I live to be a hundred, I'll never understand."

Joe resumed his reading:

. . . I would have remained a prisoner, just like you said. Not behind a wall, but in my own mind, and that would have been far worse. Deep down, I knew it all the time, but you were the one who helped me admit it. Nobody else understood or cared.

Thanks for setting me free. Come see me sometime if you get a chance; I'll be here.

Billy G.
State Prison

1

Part I
Interviewing

Lasers, DNA analysis, and other high-tech procedures have recently bombarded the world of law enforcement. Through their use, some criminals who might have remained free have gone to jail. Not surprisingly, such cases often receive extensive publicity and, unfortunately, tend to overshadow reality. Investigators, not scientists, solve the vast majority of crimes, and they do so because "somebody talked." Witnesses, accomplices, or the criminals themselves usually provide the solutions—solutions that are not obtainable through any high-tech process.

However, criminals rarely come forth voluntarily to provide these solutions, and witnesses often have no enthusiasm for becoming involved. Despite this, law enforcement agencies still manage to obtain these truly spectacular, but unpublicized results, and they do so through the efforts of a few investigators who have learned how to interview. Increasing law enforcement's cadre of competent interviewers will do more to solve crimes than any technological advance ever will.

Despite the track record of investigators solving cases through interviewing, few agencies place much emphasis on the development of the skills involved in interviewing. They offer many reasons for this policy of indifference, and each explanation has an element of truth sufficient to sustain it. However, scrutiny of these reasons will dispel their validity and expose them for what they are: Myths. These myths range from the philosophical, such as assuming that good interviewers are born, not made, to the tactical, such as believing that interviews consist solely of questions and answers. We must eliminate these myths as a first step in expanding the pool of competent interviewers.

The fictional Sergeant Joe Friday of Dragnet has probably had a more detrimental impact on police interviewing than any other single person or event. Though greatly admired as an individual, Friday's technique of insisting on "just the facts," despite its entertainment value, was poor interviewing. Unfortunately, many officers, rookies and veterans alike, imitate this style, not because it is effective, but because it is easy. By refusing to acknowledge a person's feelings and emotions, and instead just discussing the facts, the investigator removes much of the stress from interviewing. However, failure to deal with these feelings can also prevent the interviewer from obtaining those precious facts. Fear, anger, grief, and many other emotions serve as barriers to communication. If you deal with and remove these barriers, the facts will come. If they are ignored, the facts may remain unknown.

Many accomplished investigators define an interview as "a conversation with a purpose"—a definition that conflicts with the widely held myth that interviewing consists of asking a list of carefully prepared questions and meticulously recording the answers. Trying to conduct an interview in this preset way closely resembles the ploy of the nervous suitor who, before his first date, prepares a list of things to talk about. Not only does this tactic rarely succeed, it provides the material of which situation comedies are made. A conversation involves spontaneity and flexibility, qualities that are eliminated by the use of prepared questions.

The belief that interviewers are born, not made, and its counterpart belief, that interviewing can only be learned through experience, account for many investigators receiving little or no interviewing training. With few exceptions, each generation of investigators begins anew, having profited little from the experiences of the previous generation. The observation that "those who do not learn from the past are condemned to repeat it" often applies to interviewing.

Furthermore, not only do few investigators learn from history, they often even fail to benefit from their own mistakes. Only by identifying and analyzing their errors can investigators prevent their recurrence and become better interviewers; unfortunately, many have neither the knowledge nor the attitude needed to do this. Often, only training can remedy these shortcomings.

The following account of a "routine" arrest in which I took part as a rookie agent shows just how wrong things can go. Everybody involved in law enforcement has a similar story—this just happens to be mine. I confess that I have included it in part because I like to tell the story, but also because it helps to refute the common assumption that involvement in such a "comedy of errors" automatically teaches many lessons to the participants, an assumption not always borne out by experience. Participating in such an operation does not guarantee improvement any more than conducting a bad interview automatically makes one a better interviewer. We often ignore our mistakes, even those as blatant as the following:

> Through the alertness of a small-town deputy sheriff, the FBI had identified a man who had robbed a bank in an adjacent town the previous day. The deputy had noticed a stranger in town using a pay phone and, after hearing the description of the suspect, realized that he had seen him. Telephone records for the time in question, coupled with other information, led to an arrest warrant for the suspect.

> After determining that the suspect had not returned home for several days, the FBI interviewed his wife. She said that although she had no proof that her husband robbed the bank, she believed he had the capacity to do so, did fit the description and did have a revolver matching the one used in the robbery. The wife also believed that her husband intended to kill her.

Not surprisingly, the FBI easily obtained her cooperation. They then told her to do nothing to alert her husband of their interest in him should he contact her. Instead, they told her to comply with his wishes and notify the FBI as soon as possible. They would then handle the situation.

She telephoned the FBI at noon on the following day. Her husband had called and requested that she meet him early the next evening at a rest stop on a nearby interstate highway. He had told her to bring him some clothes and some money. (He had spent the entire proceeds from the robbery on a new automobile for himself and a house trailer for his girlfriend.) This advance warning provided ample time for the FBI to plan for his arrest.

Following the idea that a simple plan works best, the FBI placed a four-agent apprehension team in an old panel truck and parked it near a telephone booth at the rest stop. The wife, as instructed, parked her car beyond the phone booth so that her husband would have to drive past the agents to get to her location. The plan called for the case agent, while pretending to use the phone, to serve as a lookout. Upon the arrival of the suspect, the case agent intended to get into the truck, notify the arrest team and then drive to a point that would block the suspect's escape. The arrest team then would exit the panel truck and take the suspect into custody. Numerous FBI agents and local officers were dispersed throughout the area to serve as backups for the arrest team. They posted me on the fringe of the action about 15 miles away and told me to remain alert. For what, I never quite figured out.

The suspect, unaware of the plan, failed to fulfill his part. At the appointed hour, instead of driving into the entrance of the rest stop, he continued past it. He stopped at the exit to the rest area, backed up to his wife's car and shouted for her to follow him. He then sped from the location. His wife, as directed by the FBI, followed him. The case agent observed this from the telephone booth and, realizing that the arrest plan had failed, decided to improvise. He got into the truck, started the engine and began to give chase. At the same time, he shouted this latest development to the arrest team in the cargo area. The truck had no windows in this compartment, and they had to depend on the driver to keep them advised of the situation.

However, because of a partition between the driver and the cargo area and the loud roar of the engine, they could only guess what was happening. They knew only that the plan had failed. Although equipped with a portable radio, they could not notify the backup units of this development because the radio signals could not penetrate the walls of the panel truck.

Meanwhile, the case agent, giving chase down the interstate, attained a top speed of about 30 miles per hour. Knowing this would not catch the suspect in his new V-8-powered sedan and theorizing that the parking brake was responsible for the lack of speed, he attempted to disengage it. In doing so, he accidentally released the hood instead. Fortunately, the hood's hinges were located at the front of the hood rather than at the rear. Thus, the hood whose safety catch was missing, only raised about six inches at the rear rather than completely blocking the windshield. The agent, of small stature, could now either press the accelerator or peer over the hood; he could not do both at once.

Again, the case agent needed to improvise. He decided to take the first available exit, locate a telephone and notify the office of the current situation. The office could then update the backup units by radio. It took a long time to reach this exit, a long incline that crested at the edge of a huge parking lot, part of a truck stop complex. As the truck drove up the ramp, its engine died, and the truck came to a stop at the edge of the lot. As the driver looked over the partially raised hood, he saw, approximately 100 yards in front of him, the cars of the suspect and his wife. The suspect had gotten out of his car and was approaching his wife, the woman the FBI had promised to protect.

No problem. The case agent had a well-armed and enthusiastic arrest team with him. They could be heard clamoring and struggling to get out of the truck; the inside door handle did not work properly. Actually, their frantic efforts to exit had little to do with the arrest situation; a faulty exhaust system had caused the excessive noise made by the truck during the chase; the arrest team was being asphyxiated. What had started as a "routine" arrest with more than adequate personnel had deteriorated to a one-on-one confrontation at 100 yards between an armed and dangerous suspect and an agent with a snub-nosed revolver, a weapon designed for close-range shooting.

Fortunately, when the case agent pointed his revolver at the suspect and shouted, "Halt in the name of the FBI," the suspect froze.

Meanwhile, the arrest team, having escaped from the truck and recovered from the exhaust fumes, rushed to the suspect and placed him under arrest. As one of the backup units who had finally figured out what was happening, I arrived a few minutes later and furnished handcuffs to the arrest team. Being new, I thought everybody involved in the arrest had a pair of handcuffs. However, each arrest team member had assumed that others would have handcuffs; none did.

The next day, a newspaper account of the arrest indicated that the suspect's capture had occurred without incident. Obviously, no reporter witnessed this event. Only those involved knew the truth, and they chose not to reveal it. The agents did apprehend the suspect, but hardly "without incident." People involved in operations that go awry often edit their press releases to omit the embarrassing parts. However, a problem occurs later when they begin to believe their edited press clippings. Smugness and complacency can result.

Fortunately, most tactical units in law enforcement now conduct post-action evaluations as standard practice. They examine missions in terms of planning, equipment, and execution, and find ways to improve. Tactical units identify and analyze their mistakes and therefore tend not to repeat them. For instance, if they had reviewed the above operation they might have made the following observations:

- always review plans
- test vehicles beforehand, including:

    top speed
    exhaust system
    door and hood latches

- check communications under operational conditions
- inventory all equipment in advance

Although press releases rarely follow, interviews do not differ from tactical situations regarding the need for post-action evaluations. Only by careful analysis of past performances can interviewers improve. Otherwise, they will make the same mistakes again and again until they become ingrained—experience does not guarantee competence. The existence of many ineffective "old-timers" amply illustrates this.

"Why didn't somebody tell me this stuff years ago?" Hearing this question many times from experienced agents and police officers convinced me to write this book. In this book, as in the training course that prompted this question, I have tried to dispel some of the mystery surrounding the interview process by sharing techniques and ideas that others have used successfully through the years. I hope that this will prevent the reader from having to learn them all the hard way, through trial and error, an impossible task for one lifetime. I offer this book only as a starting point, however, not as a substitute for training, more extensive texts, or experience.

Chapter 1
Structure of an Interview

Evaluations of interviews must extend beyond merely rating them on a pass/fail basis. Interviewers must critique their efforts in performance terms: What they did or failed to do, and how to improve. To do this effectively and consistently, they must have a frame of reference against which to judge their efforts.

Fortunately, the interview process does not consist of a series of random questions or a stream-of-consciousness process. Despite the uniqueness of each interview, most good ones follow a definite structure. Interviewers can use this proven format to evaluate their own efforts, thus learning from their mistakes.

Step One—Preparation

Often ignored and frequently misunderstood, a lack of thorough preparation contributes to many interviewing failures. Consider the investigator who finds in his or her in-basket a directive to interview a minor figure regarding knowledge of a crime. The directive included a summary of the case and the reasons for the interview. Noting that on this day the investigator will be in the vicinity of the address given on other business, he puts the directive in his briefcase on the chance that he will have time to conduct this interview.

Case Facts

After completing his previously scheduled work and finding himself near the address listed on the directive, he decides to get this interview out of the way. After introducing himself and entering the residence, he rummages through his briefcase. He finds the directive and, while scanning it, mutters half to himself, half to the other person, "Now let's see here, just what is it they want me to ask you?" His question doomed the interview. With his opening remarks, the investigator has shown that he has no personal interest in this matter and has not even bothered to discover the purpose of the interview. He knows nothing about the case.

Most investigators would have prepared better than this; they at least would have reviewed the facts of the case. Unfortunately, equating case knowledge with adequate preparation causes many interviewers to fail. Numerous other short-comings in preparation contribute to failure. An infinite number of variables exist for each interview, many of which are beyond the control of the interviewer. However, interviewers should control the variables they can control.

People Facts

In the preceding scenario, not only did the investigator not know the purpose of the interview, he knew nothing about the person he intended to interview. Interviewing requires *interaction*, and knowing something about the other person can help. Has the person been interviewed before, been arrested before, or been the victim of a crime, or is he or she possibly wanted for a crime right now? The interviewer could have answered these and other related questions through a routine file search before the interview. Consider the possible consequences of the following situation had sheer luck not intervened:

Joe: I'm glad that you have a guy to interview in the same town where I have a lead to arrest another one. This way we can kill two birds with one stone.

Fred: Yeah, besides, it's a long drive alone. We can do my interview first and then try to find your guy. What did your guy do and where is he wanted?

Joe: He's a drug dealer out of Dallas. Who asked you to do your interview?

Fred: Same place, our Dallas office. That's a coincidence. Where is your guy supposed to be?

Joe: Working at the furniture factory. How about yours?

Fred: Mine too, what is your guy's name?

The answer to this question will reveal that both investigators were talking about the same person. In this case, failure to adequately search the files nearly resulted in a very embarrassing and dangerous situation.

Does the person own a home or have a job? Who lives with him or her, and who are his or her neighbors? In most locations, this information appears in a readily available city directory or other reference. Do not make a "federal case" out of preparation, but do not ignore the obvious; know about the person to be interviewedbeforehand.

> **Think of each interview as a first date; leave nothing to chance.**

Timing

Schedule the interview for optimum effectiveness; often, no second chance will occur. What time of day? A potential suspect or witness may be known to have a three-martini lunch, and this could have a bearing on deciding when to do the interview. Thorough preparation may reveal whether it should take place before or after lunch. At what point in the case? If conducted prematurely, the investigator may not have the information needed to do a thorough job, but if the interview is conducted too late in the investigation, the suspect may be forewarned and forearmed. There is no best answer for all cases. However, a best answer exists for *each* case, determined by the circumstances of that case. Just being "in the neighborhood" should not dictate when to conduct an interview.

Location

Comedian Bill Cosby talks about visiting homes with small children, and he laments that social rules require that he pretend to admire them. As a result, one of them may like him and want to sit on his lap and give him a hug. Even Joe Friday might have trouble maintaining his composure in such a situation. This illustrates just one reason why the investigator should always give some thought to the location for the interview.

Interviewers can learn much about a person's values by seeing how he or she furnishes his or her office. Investigators may wish to convey a more formal and serious tone by choosing a government building or police station. A neutral site, such as a restaurant, may also provide the key to success. The relaxed atmosphere that a home provides may even overcome the distractions there. Again, the best answer exists for each case, not for every case.

Number of Interviewers

> I've got to talk with a guy in the other end of our territory—how about going with me? I could use the company, and besides, there is a good restaurant there where we can have lunch.

Investigators should always consider the number of interviewers who will participate in an interview, but not for the above reasons. Personal security may dictate the need for assistance; interviewers should never sacrifice their safety. Aside from this consideration, however, most interviews are best conducted one-on-one, particularly if the interviewer anticipates reluctance on the part of the subject. Interviewers often obtain the cooperation of reluctant interviewees by gaining their trust and respect. Extra people get in the way of this process. Refuting allegations of misconduct, taking notes, lending technical expertise, and many other reasons often justify the presence of a second interviewer. Absent unusual circumstances, none of these reasons supersedes the need to acquire the information, something usually best done alone.

Step Two—Introduction

Etiquette and common sense suggest the need for an introduction. This should consist of name, authority/position, and the purpose of the interview. Failure to furnish these facts makes little sense and will usually result in the interviewee asking, "Who are you and what do you want?" The interviewer becomes the interviewee from the outset.

Although a name and position leave little margin for flexibility, explaining the purpose of the interview allows a great deal of leeway. How the interviewer handles this often sets the tone for the entire interview. What tone does the following introduction set?

> I'm here to find out where your son is, lady. I'm going to arrest him for robbery and put him in jail for a long time. If you know what's good for you, you'll tell me where he is. I get very angry when people lie to me.

> **You never get a second chance to make a first impression.**

If someone talked to you like that, would it make you eager to help him or her? Nonthreatening language works better. It reduces the anxiety that law enforcement representatives trigger when they first encounter either a witness or a suspect. No advantage comes from putting a person on the defensive and heightening this anxiety by using threatening words or a threatening tone.

> Hey Fred, I'm Detective Anderson, and I'd like to talk with you about what happened the other night. I think you can probably help shed some light on the situation.

Many investigators, when meeting an individual for the first time, would use an opening statement similar to Detective Anderson's. By doing so, they have requested assistance that potential witnesses feel they can grant or refuse with equal ease, and many choose not to get involved. Interviewers should strive to make refusing to cooperate more difficult than cooperating.

One agent developed a reputation for his ability to secure the cooperation of individuals who would have nothing to do with anyone else, and his associates had difficulty understanding why. The agent seemed average in all respects, possessing neither mental nor physical attributes that would give him an advantage over his peers. He lacked a recruiter poster image by a wide margin, and observations of him in action failed to reveal any unique or astounding techniques. However, his initial approach did vary from others in one respect—he would begin by saying:

> Hey Fred, I'm Charlie Youngerman, and we need to talk about what happened last night. You've got to give your version so we can get on with this investigation.

> **Poor: "I'd like to talk with you."**
> **Better: "We need to talk because . . ."**

Subtle differences in word choices during the introduction can have a significant impact on an interview. Charlie never told people that he would like to talk with them. Instead, he used the phrase "we need to talk." By using a statement rather than a plea, he removed the option or burden for decisionmaking from the person interviewed. People can easily decline requests, but they have more difficulty with declarative statements. Charlie knew this and used it to his advantage.

Step Three—Establish Rapport

Rapport is a state of mind, and although most people recognize it, few can define it. Words such as *empathy*, *liking*, and *comfort* come close. But although the presence of these conditions may aid in developing rapport, they do not capture the essence of it.

Rapport's elusiveness stems from the requirement that two individuals achieve a state of harmony through an informal process that has no rules. In addition, the responsibility for achieving this harmonious state lies exclusively with the interviewer, whose mere presence produces feelings of anxiety in the interviewee.

Reduce Anxiety

Fortunately for investigators, many interviewees wish to cooperate, but this does not preclude the need for establishing rapport. Cooperation does make it easier, however, because many interviewees will help in this process. They do so by providing the interviewer with opportunities to create a harmonious atmosphere.

The following demonstrates how this can work:

As the Assistant Senior Agent in Montpelier, Vermont, I had the opportunity to conduct many pre-employment background investigations—the office had only two agents, and the senior agent chose not to do these investigations. During these investigations, I interviewed many neighbors of prospective employees. The most common response received from these neighbors, one that came after I had introduced myself but had yet to explain my purpose, was, "I didn't do it!" This statement, often accompanied with a raising of the hands and taking a step backward, came from people who knew that nobody suspected them of anything. Their reactions made no sense to me and caused me some concern until I realized they were joking due to their nervousness. I eventually learned to reply in an exaggerated, stone-faced manner, "that's what they all say." This worked because I had responded in kind. They had been joking and so was I. They had given me an opportunity to reduce, through humor, the anxiety that a visit from a law enforcement agent creates.

Flattery

Quite by accident, I discovered another technique that contributes to rapport development: Make people feel better about themselves and they will attribute this feeling to you. This was not a new discovery; man has known this since the beginning of recorded time.

The accident that led to my discovery resulted from the FBI's decision to issue new credentials to all of its agents. This occurred shortly after J. Edgar Hoover's death, and his successor had relaxed the organization's grooming standards. The new rules permitted agents to wear colored shirts and to grow mustaches, so I bought a few of the former, and I grew the latter shortly before they took my photograph for the new credentials. I quickly became disenchanted with this new look, and by the time my moustache-bearing credentials arrived, I had shaved it off. I gave little thought to this discrepancy until about four months later when, during an introduction, I showed my credentials, and to my surprise, a woman said to me, "You've shaved off your moustache." I looked at my credentials and immediately responded, "You know, you're right, and although I did that months ago, you're the first person to have noticed it." A perceptible change occurred; her self-esteem increased. She obviously had better powers of observation than most, and I had noted it. Therefore, I must not be such a bad guy.

Few people examine credentials closely—they look but do not see. Therefore, I modified my method of presenting them. Instead of briefly flashing them and returning them to my pocket, I would continue to display them until nearly everyone interviewed would note, "You shaved your moustache," or something to that effect. I would immediately respond with surprise, "You know, you're right, and although I did that about six months ago, you're one of the first people to notice it." The same effect happened nearly every time, and rapport development had begun.

The caveat of this and similar techniques results from the need for perceived sincerity. Otherwise people will regard you as someone they cannot trust.

> **Sincerity is the key to success; when you can fake that, you've got it made.**
> *George Burns*

The above techniques, and an infinite number of others, although they do not constitute rapport, do aid in its development by providing a "foot in the door." They offer investigators the opportunity to demonstrate through subsequent words and demeanor that they will proceed fairly and competently. When the interviewee reaches this conclusion, rapport exists.

What kinds of words and demeanor offer the best chance of causing people to reach this conclusion? It depends on the nature of the inquiry and on the person being interviewed. There is no magic formula suitable for all occasions. There is, however, a best approach for each person and each set of circumstances.

Mirroring

"I'd be happy to come to your party next Saturday. What should I wear?" The desire to fit in, to be accepted, causes most of us to ask such questions. New spring fashions appear. Women flock to buy skirts of a different length, men buy ties of a different width and color scheme, and teenagers, despite their desire for individuality, end up dressing alike.

People strive for this because they are more comfortable when they are "in sync" with their peers, and they will go to great effort and expense to achieve this effect. Failure to do so can cause their peers to regard them as eccentric or even as freaks—not a comfortable role for most people.

More than 20 years ago, Robert Bandler and John Grinder, researchers who were examining the techniques of many psychotherapists, found that one commonality among successful therapists was the ability to get "in sync" with their patients. It enhanced communication and improved results. As a result, Bandler and Grinder developed a behavior modification process that they called *neuro-linguistic programming,* which concentrated on achieving harmony, not through dress and hairstyle, but through words and actions. In so doing, they modeled their behavior on the performances of their colleagues whom they regarded as effective communicators.

Bandler and Grinder noted what seems obvious: That different people display different mannerisms and degrees of dynamics when interacting with others. They also noted the not-so-obvious—that most successful communicators tended to duplicate, or "mirror," the mannerisms and dynamics of those with whom they dealt. Animated, rapid-speaking people seemed to communicate best with other animated, rapid-speaking people. Conversely, sedate, measured-speaking individuals responded best to those who acted like them.

> **A topic of mutual interest does not guarantee rapport.**

"I can't put my finger on it, but I'm getting some bad vibes about that guy." These good or bad "vibes" that defy further description might depend upon the degree of synchronization developed during the conversation. Posture, body movement, speech rate, and rate and depth of breathing may all contribute to these "vibrations."

A polygrapher conducted an experiment to confirm the rapport-developing aspects of mirroring. During his many airline trips, he would seat himself in the terminal diagonally across from the person he had chosen for the experiment. Although not face-to-face, each could see the other via peripheral vision or a slight turn of the head. The polygrapher would, on one-half of these occasions, attempt to mirror the unsuspecting travelers, by adopting their posture, duplicating their gestures, and displaying similar amounts of interest in the surrounding activities. On the other occasions, he deliberately avoided any mirroring behavior.

On each occasion, he noted whether the other traveler would initiate conversation with him. He found that those whom he mirrored were more apt to ask: "What flight are you taking?" or "Been here long?" or another opening line. His observations have relevance not only for the professional interviewer but may also apply in other fields.

Another aspect related to mirroring that Bandler and Grinder examined involved language. They found that different people tend to express themselves differently; they use different words and do so with some consistency. For instance, in response to a teacher's inquiry regarding the clarity of a lesson, one student might respond, "I get the picture," another may say, "That sounds right to me," and a third may answer, "I feel pretty good about it."

Although they all responded positively, each used a different mode of expression. The first used a visual reference, "picture," the second used an auditory reference, "sounds," and the third used a kinesthetic term, "feel."

If asked a similar question at another time, they would tend to answer it using the same modes of expression as they did at first. Although able to comprehend any of the terms used, people seem to have dominant or preferred modes of speech and do not usually jump randomly from visual to auditory to kinesthetic phraseology unless the topic mandates it.

Bandler and Grinder concluded that, by noting the dominant mode of a person and then mirroring it, interviewers can contribute significantly to the rapport-developing process. They based this on the premise that a person's dominant mode does not merely reflect a preference for specific words but also indicates the person's thought process. If a person says that he or she "sees what you mean," or "gets the picture," he or she is literally describing their mind's activity; they visualize their thoughts. Those who "hear what you're saying" think in words or sounds, not pictures. People who "feel pretty good" about something do just that—they feel.

For example, in response to a question or cue regarding a thunderstorm, the visual person probably "sees" a flash of lightning, the auditory person "hears" the clap of thunder, and the kinesthetic person "feels" the wind or rain hitting the face. As a result, asking auditory types how an idea looks to them may cause some difficulty. They do not know how it *looks* because they do not *see* it. Therefore, they must first translate the question to their mode of thinking: "He is asking me how it sounds." Any time that people must translate before thinking, communication suffers. Force people to do this often enough and communication ceases. Therefore, interviewers should determine, and then use, the interviewee's preferred language style.

Determining a person's dominant mode might seem to require a lot of time, which is not always available to the hard-pressed investigator. Indeed, it might require quite a bit of listening to confidently reach a conclusion regarding a person's preferred mode of expression. Fortunately, an interviewer can detect a person's dominant mode by watching him or her as well as by listening.

The eyes provide the key. Generally speaking, left-brained individuals, who make up about 90 percent of the population, display the following eye movements when searching their memories. Visual people look up and left at a 45-degree angle. Auditory people look directly left. Kinesthetic people look down and right at a 45-degree angle. Right-brained people, the other 10 percent, display a mirror image of their left-brained counterparts. The visuals look up and to the right; the auditories look directly to the right, and the kinesthetics look down and to the left.

To determine a person's dominant mode of thought, an interviewer need only observe his or her subject's eye movements during a few minutes of conversation. This conversation must deal with topics that require the subjects to search their memories; questions they can answer spontaneously, such as "What are your name and address?" will not suffice. "Tell me about your favorite vacation" probably will. Once determined, the interviewer should strive to steep as much of the conversation as possible in the subject's dominant mode because people will appreciate it, even if on a subconscious level.

No matter what techniques interviewers use to develop rapport or how long it takes, they must do it before advancing to the next step of the interview. It is like painting a house; the scraping and sanding must be done first, even if this seems to require a disproportionate amount of the total time of the interview. Also, once an interviewer develops rapport with a subject, he or she must maintain it. Rapport is dynamic. It can change, and it can disappear. If it does, the interviewer must reestablish it before the interview can proceed.

Step Four—Questions

When interviewing crime victims, few investigators begin with questions such as: "How tall was the subject?" "What color was his hair?" "Did he have any scars?" Common sense, experience, and training lead investigators to the conclusion that such specific questions give witnesses little opportunity to tell what they know. Open-ended questions produce better results. A question such as, "What did he look like?" eliminates the need for investigators to anticipate every descriptive detail that victims may have noticed. Investigators can always follow up the witness' statement with specific, direct questions to fill in gaps. But what happens when even the direct questions fail to produce the details from the witness?

> **When a witness tells you a suspect was tall, resist the urge to ask, "How tall?"**

Consider the following scenario: At a robbery scene, a uniformed officer briefs the investigating detective. Hoping to obtain additional information, the detective approaches the victim, a clerk, introduces himself and, sensing her anxiety, takes some time to assure her that she has nothing to worry about. He tells her that he understands the trauma she has just undergone, gets her a cup of coffee, and delays asking any questions until she has regained her composure. He then tells her that he needs her help and asks that she start at the beginning and tell him exactly what happened. She replies:

> I was behind the counter when all of a sudden, I heard a voice telling me to give him all the money, and I would not get hurt. I looked up and saw a man wearing a ski mask, pointing a gun right at me. I just froze and stared at the gun. He told me to get a move on or there would be trouble. I opened the cash register and handed him all of the bills. There was just under $100 in the register. He then told me to lay on the floor and not move. I did as he told me and waited until I was sure he was gone. I yelled to Joe, the manager, who was in the office, who asked me if I was okay. He then ran to the phone and called the police. The next thing I knew, the police officer arrived, and I told him the same thing I just told you. I don't know what the guy looked like, where he came from, or how he got away. I'm sorry I can't be more helpful.

The detective tells her she has been very helpful and that now he would like to go over the story again, and this time, if she does not mind, he will interrupt her with questions as she goes along. As she retells her story, he constantly probes for additional details, such as the possibility of additional witnesses, more descriptive data regarding the subject and his weapon, words he may have used, noticeable accent, and his means of escape. However, except for a bit more descriptive data, the victim was correct; she had told the responding officer everything she could remember.

The previous scenario illustrates a problem encountered by many investigators. That problem results not from the investigator's inability to ask good questions but simply from a witness who cannot provide the answers. Responses such as, "I don't remember," "That's all I saw," or "I can't recall," routinely frustrate many interviewers.

In the past, this problem led investigators to try hypnosis as a means of enhancing witness recall. Improved results confirmed what many investigators suspected—the main problem resulted, not from a lack of witness observations, but from the inability to remember what they had seen. Although investigators achieved some success through hypnosis, those successes did not last long. Courts regularly began ruling in favor of defense attorneys who alleged that hypnosis tainted any information obtained through that technique—that it often yielded facts suggested by the hypnotist rather than information recalled by the witness. As a result, investigators now primarily reserve hypnosis for situations in which the need for information supersedes all other considerations. They know that using hypnosis will probably disqualify a witness from testifying.

The Cognitive Interview: An Innovative Approach to Questioning

To enhance witness recall without the stigma attached to hypnosis, Ronald P. Fisher of Florida International University and Edward Geiselman of UCLA, have developed a system they call the *cognitive interview*. Although their process contains few, if any, new ideas, they have systematized techniques that investigators have for the most part used only in a sporadic, piecemeal fashion. Research suggests that the cognitive approach to interviewing witnesses increases the quantity of information obtained and, unlike hypnosis, it does not jeopardize the witness' credibility in court.

Specific memory-enhancing techniques used in the cognitive interview that are not part of most traditional interviews include:

- reinstating the context of the event
- recalling the event in a different sequence
- looking at the event from a different perspective

Traditional interviews of victims and witnesses, similar to the one previously described, usually begin with interviewers first taking the time to make introductions and to put witnesses at ease before asking, "What happened?" or

"What can you tell me about . . .?" They then ask specific questions geared to filling in the gaps inadvertently left by the witnesses. Proponents of the cognitive interview suggest this usually will not produce optimum results. Asking people to isolate events in their minds and then to verbalize those events requires them to operate in a vacuum. Even without the trauma that often results from involvement or victimization in a crime, a person's memory functions better when things are put into context. Using the cognitive interview contributes to this process.

> **Did you ever find your car keys by mentally retracing your steps? Help witnesses use the same process.**

Reinstate the Context

What do Fisher and Geiselman mean by context and how can interviewers establish it? Simply put, interviewers must make efforts to reestablish the environment, mood, setting, and experiences by asking witnesses to mentally relive the events that occurred before, during, and after the crime.

Let's return to the previously described robbery scene with the detective who had already introduced himself to the victim and asked for her help. Instead of asking her what happened during the crime, he might proceed as follows, using the cognitive interview:

> It's only about 10:00 in the morning and it's already been a pretty full day for you. How about telling me how your day started? Tell me what time you got up, the chores you did, the errands you ran and anything else that happened before you came to work.

> **Reset the victim's mood as well as the scene.**

As she recounts her activities, the detective joins the conversation, discussing events with her, including the problems of a working mother, what she fixed for breakfast, and any other details that she mentions. Only when they have developed a clear picture of those events does the detective suggest that the victim describe her travel to work. He handles this portion of the conversation in the same way. He does not ask perfunctory questions geared to getting her quickly to the crime scene, but rather, he discusses her commute to work in-depth. They talk about the route she took, the weather and traffic conditions she encountered, events she may have seen, and finally, where she parked her car and what she noticed at that time. He wants her not just to describe her day, but to relive it.

He uses the same interview technique regarding her arrival at work. By the time they finally get to the discussion of the robbery, they have put the event into context; it is not the sole event of the day. Often, this process enhances a person's ability to remember. The witness can put details of the robbery into perspective and thus concentrate and focus better than during any previous interviews that consisted of isolated questions and answers. The response, "I can't remember," will occur less frequently.

Change the Order of Events

To continue the interview and further develop the witness' recall, the interviewer may follow with another phase of the cognitive interview. Usually, a witness retrieves information from his or her memory chronologically. However, when recounting information in this way, people tend to edit as they tell the story. This results in a summary based upon what the witness regards as important. Although interviewers often try to remedy this problem by telling witnesses not to hold back even the most insignificant detail, most interviewers can cite instances in which valuable information went unmentioned because a witness chose to omit it. Interviewers should devote significant effort to encouraging their witnesses to tell all. However, usually this only reduces rather than eliminates the tendency to edit.

One technique that contributes to reduced editing requires the witness to tell his or her story other than in chronological order. By changing the sequence of recall and asking the witness to tell his or her story backward, the interviewer can prompt the witness to look at each stage of the event as a separate entity—much akin to looking at the individual frames of a motion picture. Reverse or out-of-order recall also encourages overly zealous witnesses to stick to the facts. Witnesses find it more difficult to embellish an account when they separate themselves from the natural flow of events and deal independently with each activity.

Returning to the eyewitness interview in the opening scenario, the detective might continue using the cognitive interview technique. Accordingly, he would discuss the conversation the victim had with the responding officer and ask where she was when the officer arrived. He wants to know exactly what she was doing at that time. What did she do immediately before that and before that? Through this line of questioning, he gradually goes back to the time of the robbery. Thus, he leads her through a second recounting of the crime, only in reverse. This time she has recalled her information as a collection of pieces viewed independently. Just as looking at a portion of the landscape may reveal details missed while taking in the panoramic view, looking at the stages of an event in reverse may enable witnesses to "see" previously unnoticed items.

Change Perspective

To further stimulate witnesses' memories, Fisher and Geiselman also suggest changing the perspective. A witness experiences an event only once. However, he or she may perceive it from various views. During initial recollection, witnesses usually recount from their personal perspectives and rarely stray from that point of view. By prompting a witness to physically change the positioning in his or her memory, the interviewer gives him or her the opportunity to recall more of his or her experience. Interviewers can change the witness' perspective by asking him or her to consider the view of another witness, victim, or an invisible eye on the wall.

> **Help the witness avoid tunnel vision.**

Using the technique of changing perspective, the detective in the opening scenario might say:

> You know those surveillance cameras they have in banks and some stores? Too bad there wasn't one on the wall over there. I wonder just what it would have recorded; it certainly would have had a different vantage point than you did.

Through this opening statement, he can draw the victim into a discussion of what might have been recorded on the nonexistent camera. This technique not only provides her with an opportunity to "replay" the event from a different angle, but also further defuses the trauma of the situation. Reviewing a film produces less anxiety than reliving an armed robbery.

Techniques of Specific Retrieval

Depending on the circumstances, interviewers may use additional techniques to promote memory retrieval. After a witness has recounted an event in its natural sequence, reverse sequence, and from different perspectives, the interviewer can prompt specific retrieval by asking direct questions. One technique of specific retrieval includes associating witnesses' recollections of physical appearance, clothing, and sounds with something or someone familiar to them. Interviewers may enhance other areas of recall, such as names and license plates, by dealing with individual components of the items, such as the first letter or number. Once established, interviewers direct concentration to the next letter or number and develop the answer one item at a time.

Using this technique, the detective in the robbery scenario might review the details obtained thus far and, at certain points, stop to ask questions such as:

> "You say he had a scary voice. How so? Does it remind you of anybody you know, or perhaps somebody you've seen in a movie? The coveralls he was wearing—ever seen that type before? Where? Were they like a pilot's flight suit, or more like a carpenter's outfit?"

Poor: How ugly was he?
Better: Ugly like whom?

This context-enhancing technique stems from realizing that the victim did not experience this event as a clean slate. Instead, she had a lifetime of experiences that preceded it. Therefore, when obtaining a description of the subject, a detective's questions, "Does this person remind you of anyone you know? In what way?" provide a context from which the victim can make comparisons. This removes her need to create by enabling her to draw on information she already has.

The cognitive interview often helps witnesses recall more information by forcing interviewers to avoid traps normally associated with "routine" interviewing, specifically, rushing the witness and interrupting his or her account. Witnesses must feel confident that they have time to think, speak, reflect, and speak again without annoying impatient investigators. Interviewers can instill this confidence by allowing sufficient time for the interview and by refraining from interrupting witnesses. All too often interviewers say, "Tell me what happened," but almost immediately thereafter, begin asking specific questions. This rushes the witness, frustrates him or her and encourages brevity. If they are not given enough time, the witness cannot concentrate or remember.

The cognitive interview technique not only enhances witness recall, it also addresses another problem that is common among interviewers—an inability to sustain the interview. Investigators, particularly inexperienced investigators, often find themselves saying, "I can't think of anything else to ask. Is there anything you're leaving out?" If the witness says, "No," the interview is over. Using the cognitive technique can help interviewers avoid reaching this point prematurely. Experience shows that the cognitive technique allows interviewers to continue discussing events without feeling or sounding redundant. This continued conversation often prompts additional recall.

The cognitive interview can also apply outside the investigative world. For example, one student at the FBI Academy recently had reason to thank an instructor for teaching some cognitive interview techniques. Before leaving for home on a Friday afternoon, this student had asked his roommate to pick him up at the airport the following Sunday. The roommate agreed to do so, but unfortunately, although he remembered his promise, he could not recall any of the details such as the time of arrival, the airline, nor even which airport. He voiced this problem to a fellow student, who said:

> I just learned about this retrieval technique in interviewing, maybe it will help. What time did you get up on Friday? Tell me what you did after that.

Starting from this point, he walked the forgetful student through the morning. When they arrived at lunch time, the student remembered both the airport and the airline; he was then able to figure out the plane's arrival time.

Step Five—Verification

The prosecutor, before trial, has just reread the detective's report containing the star witness' account of a very complicated conspiracy case. In final preparation for the trial, he had the detective bring the witness to the office to review the information he had furnished. As the prosecutor paraphrases the detective's version of the statement, the witness becomes increasingly uncomfortable. The detective notes this and attributes it to pretrial jitters. Finally, as the prosecutor says that the witness can testify that the defendant was the only person present during all but a couple of the relevant meetings, the witness states, "That's not what I told the detective." "Yes you did," replies the detective. "Like hell I did." replied the witness, "I told you that of all of the meetings that took place, the defendant was only at a couple of them." After several disputes about what he did or did not say, the witness shouts, "That's not what I said, and it certainly isn't what I meant."

> *Bad* can mean *good; great* can mean *awful*. You will never know for sure unless you ask.

Who is right and who is wrong? Does it really matter? The witness' testimony differs significantly from what the prosecutor expected. Why did this happen? Some explanations include:

- interviewers often hear what they want or expect to hear
- witnesses think one thing but say another
- many words mean different things to different people

> **Poor:**   **Are you sure about what you just said?**
> **Better:** **Let's see if I understand you.**

Most important, how can interviewers prevent this from happening? To do so, interviewers need only paraphrase what they think they have heard and ask the witnesses to verify its accuracy, a procedure that often goes undone. Not only will this process prevent misunderstanding, it will also provide another chance to review the information furnished, and this sometimes prompts additional recall by the witness.

Step Six—Catch-All Question

As indicated previously, reviewing the facts for verification may prompt the witness to recall other information not previously furnished. The interviewer must take advantage of this possibility by providing the witness with an opportunity to volunteer this information. During follow-up interviews, witnesses often amaze investigators by providing important, previously unknown information. In response to the question, "Why didn't you tell me that before?" often comes the reply, "You didn't ask me."

With cooperative witnesses, the catch-all question usually comes at the end of the interview and consists of wording such as, "Now that I have gone over the facts, can you think of anything else that might be of value, anything I forgot to ask?" With witnesses of questionable candor, the interviewer may want to phrase the catch-all question differently: "That is what you have told me so far, now how about telling me the rest of the story?" This question conveys two unspoken messages: "You have not told me the whole truth," and "This interview is not over."

Step Seven—Departure

Just as interviewers must develop rapport before asking questions and maintain this atmosphere during questioning, they must also sustain it afterward. Creating the impression that the interviewer appreciated their efforts will encourage witnesses to recontact the interviewer if they later recall some additional information. Conversely, interviewers must create an atmosphere that will make them welcome if they return, either to ask additional questions or to summon the person to appear as a witness. Statements such as: "If you think of anything else, give me a call," and, "What's the best way to get back in touch with you if I need to talk to you again?" do much to set this tone.

> **When leaving, don't slam the door;**
> **you might have to come back.**

Even after conducting unsuccessful interviews, investigators should avoid needlessly creating a feeling of ill will. "Thanks a lot, you jerk," although it may produce a momentary feeling of satisfaction, has no place in the interview process. It also makes rapport building much more difficult if a second interview is required.

Step Eight—Critique

"If I were to do that interview over again, what would I do differently?" Asking yourself this question provides the chance for improvement, whether confronting a bank robbery suspect or interviewing a crime victim. Unfortunately, many conscientious interviewers who willingly ask this question often have trouble answering it. They are left with vague feelings of inadequacy but no solution. This often results from looking at the interview holistically, which is adequate for providing a rating, but not for enhancing performance. Novice marksmen can identify with this dilemma. By scoring their targets, they learn that they have shortcomings, but this does not correct the shortcomings. Only by systematically analyzing the individual fundamentals of shooting such as grip, trigger squeeze, sight alignment, and sight picture can shooters identify their problems and find the solutions.

> **Experience is the best teacher only**
> **if you learn from your mistakes.**

Critiques of interviews must follow the same analysis process, or improvement will not occur. "Did I prepare properly? Did I develop and maintain rapport, ask open-ended questions, listen, and verify the answers?" These and similar questions, based on the proven structure of the interview, will produce improvement; merely noting mistakes will not. As a school principal once noted about his staff, "Some of my teachers have 20 years' experience, others have one year's experience—20 times." Repetition and experience are not synonymous.

Summary

Although each interview is unique, most successful interviews follow a pattern consisting of a series of steps, starting with preparation and progressing through introduction, rapport building, questions, verification, catch-all, depature, and critique. This pattern not only serves as a road map for the interviewer to follow, it provides a benchmark that the interviewer can use to evaluate each interview, to identify mistakes, and thus to avoid repeating them.

Suggested Reading

Bandler, Robert and John Grinder (1979). *Frogs into Princes: Neuro-Linguistic Programming*. Moab, UT: Real People Press.

Cheatham, T. Richard and Keith V. Erickson (1984). *The Police Officer's Guide to Better Communications*. Glenview, IL: Scott, Foresman and Company.

Fisher, Ronald P. and Edward Geiselman (1992). *Memory-Enhancing Techniques for Investigative Interviewing: The Cognitive Interview*. Springfield, IL: Charles C Thomas.

O'Connor, Joseph and John Seymour (1995). *Introducing Neuro-Linguistic Programming*. San Francisco, CA: Thorsons.

Chapter 2
Demeanor

Most aspiring investigators understand much of the material discussed in Chapter 1. They also know that this understanding does not ensure success. Despite some experience, many are still looking for the answer to the question they asked as rookies: "How does a good interviewer act?" They want to know what behavior distinguishes the proficient from the mediocre.

Trainers often try to address the question regarding behavior with the following guidance:

> When you get out there on the street, you have to dominate the situation. I don't care if you are interviewing a reference in an applicant matter or interrogating a dangerous felon, you have to dominate the situation. You must be in charge.

Unfortunately, despite the wisdom of this advice, unless trainers explain how to achieve this dominance, and few do, it has little value. Instead, they leave the trainees to interpret this directive for themselves. As a result, many rookies base their behavior on a role model taken from the media. In the 1970s, Kojak, a glib, abrasive, television detective from New York City, who seemed to control situations through arrogance, provided a typical example of how one could "dominate the situation." Each succeeding generation has had its own similar role model.

Most rookie interviewers who try to emulate the "Kojak" style of dominance fail. Rather than dominating, they usually create hostility because few people, innocent or guilty, appreciate this type of treatment. Rookies, in turn, respond to the hostility by escalating their arrogance and, ultimately, a confrontation occurs—not the desired effect.

Others fail to achieve dominance in a less offensive but equally ineffective fashion. Rather than irritating others, they amuse them. Placing people in positions of authority and then causing them to behave in inappropriate ways has served as the basis for several popular television programs. Deputy Barney Fife of *The Andy Griffith Show* illustrates this. He attempted to assert his authority by strutting around and announcing "I am in charge." However, those who must announce their authority do not have it and, typically do not possess such skills or credibility. Actions, not words, determine dominance, as demonstrated by a

29

shaken and unauthorized Secretary of State Alexander Haig (who resigned in 1982), following the 1981 assassination attempt on President Ronald Reagan:

> As of this moment, I am in charge.

If neither Kojak nor Barney Fife is an acceptable role model, rookies must look elsewhere. If they decide to choose from role models offered by television, they could select the character of detective lieutenant Columbo. His consistent behavior over a 20-year history, although viewed as inept by the casual observer, epitomizes the actions of a truly dominant investigator.

The seemingly bumbling detective Columbo had a propensity for returning to the suspect for additional information. After asking a few mundane questions, he would begin to leave. However, just as he got to the door, he would pause, turn, and ask "just one more question." He would ask this "one more question" not to obtain information but to let the suspect know the case was not closed.

Only when viewed in the context of dominance does the true nature of Columbo emerge. He has mastered dominance, but neither the audience nor his adversaries realize this. Much of the audience thinks he is feigning stupidity, and his opponents regard him as a buffoon. Both assessments miss the mark.

To understand Columbo's technique, one can examine any episode. Each has a variation of the same routine. In each case, Columbo will repeatedly return to the suspect's domain and, on each visit, will add to the suspect's discomfort. Not only his presence, but his demeanor while there, contribute to this discomfort.

Whatever the episode, the suspect will be a part of the elite of some field such as industry or show business and will usually be the sophisticated type. When Columbo arrives to talk with him or her yet again, the suspect, wearing an expensive suit, sitting behind an expensive desk in a large, well-appointed office, will exude power.

Contrast this with detective Columbo, who appears at the door in his trademark wrinkled raincoat. The remainder of his clothing is rumpled and mismatched. He needs a haircut and a shave, and has a bewildered look, which is exacerbated by his glass eye. His poor posture reinforces this downtrodden appearance. His words, indicative of submission, also contribute to this overall effect. They imply that he will conform to the suspect's schedule due to the relative importance of the suspect and because only a few petty details have caused him to return for yet another interview. For example:

> I know you are a busy man, and I can always come back another time. I've just got a couple of loose ends to clear up for my report, and they can wait if you wish. I wouldn't bother you at all except that I got this new captain, and he's a nice kid and all, but he's a real stickler for details. You know what I mean?

Because the suspect has grown tired of dealing with Columbo and certainly does not want him returning again, he or she will invite him in and ask him what he wants this time. The observer must closely watch what Columbo does during this scene because his actions, not his words, provide the key. While delivering his opening monologue, Columbo, without invitation, will already have entered the office, thus rendering the suspect's invitation completely unnecessary.

Suspect:	**I'm busy, go away.**
Poor:	**I'll decide when to go.**
Better:	**That's why I'll be brief.**

Having entered the office, he will locate the suspect's prized possession, usually a priceless art object, and without hesitation, will carelessly pick it up and begin to talk about it:

> This is really lovely. You know, my wife would like something like this. She knows a lot more about sculpture than I do, but even I can see that this is a fine piece. There's a shopping center just down the road that I passed on the way up here. It has a big department store that handles all kinds of stuff. You didn't by any chance pick this up over there, did you?

By this time, the suspect will have lost all semblance of the sophistication that he showed a few minutes earlier. Not only does Columbo handle the priceless object in a cavalier way and will probably soon drop it and break it, he also insults it by implying that he might purchase a duplicate in a department store. If the suspect does not leap over his desk to get to Columbo, he immediately rushes around the desk to rescue the object and scold Columbo:

> Detective Columbo, that is very fragile so I would appreciate it if you would not handle it. It also cost about five years of your salary. It is a one-of-a-kind masterpiece and certainly cannot be purchased in a shopping center.

In response to this chastisement, Columbo will look a bit contrite and, if the suspect has not taken the object from him, will return it close to where he found it. He will rarely put it exactly where it had been, thus compelling the suspect to adjust its position. While the suspect does this, Columbo will move to another part of the room, leaving the suspect standing by himself. He will then turn his attention to something else, such as the view from the office window, and say:

Would you look at that! That is magnificent. You know, my wife paints. Did I mention to you that she paints? If she could only see this view. You don't think it might be possible sometime for her, particularly when the sun is shining just like it is now . . .

Columbo will then ramble on interminably about the view, much to the irritation of the suspect, who finally will interrupt him. The suspect, despite an effort to appear indifferent, has a desire to know just what Columbo wants this time. Viewers see this as Columbo's primary investigative technique. They do not realize that he has done much more than merely raise concern regarding the cause of his visit. His disregard for the suspect's position probably causes more aggravation than his questions do. The suspect has two items that he prizes highly, the piece of art and his time; Columbo has treated each of them with disdain. He has mishandled one and wasted the other. Even more disconcerting, he has done so with no hint of concern. He neither asked permission nor apologized in any meaningful way. He has done what people who are in charge do. Within the bounds of socially acceptable behavior, they do anything they want. People in charge do not ask permission—they do not need it.

> **Arrogance does not indicate dominance, being at ease does.**

Societies establish rules that govern the behavior of their members. Without ever receiving any formal training regarding these rules, most people know and follow them. For instance, no one ever went to school to learn elevator etiquette. However, people know that when they get on an elevator, they must press the button for their floor, face the front of the elevator, and watch the floor numbers change. Fellow passengers are uncomfortable with anyone who deviates from this behavior. People also know the rules for dominant versus subservient behavior, and most realize that violating these rules can cause problems.

Although feeling free to do as one wishes without asking permission epitomizes dominance, some specific actions and behaviors often distinguish the dominant person from the rest. People can usually identify group leaders by observation alone, and hearing their words rarely provides much additional insight. Only actions count. Those in charge feel free to invade the space of their subordinates. A supervisor can enter a staff member's office and lean on or even sit on that person's desk. Rarely will the subordinate respond in a similar way in the supervisor's office. Not only would the subordinate not sit on the desk, but he or she probably would not sit anywhere else until invited to do so. Supervisors may also feel free to peruse subordinates' displayed possessions, interrupt them at will, and talk to or ignore them as they see fit. Truly dominant individuals not only may do all of the above and many other things that subordinates would never consider, but they may do so without expecting to cause any resentment on the part of their subordinates.

In the structured worlds of the military, police departments, and private corporations, people know the "pecking order" and behave accordingly. In the world of investigation, no established hierarchy exists. Whoever displays the dominant behaviors will control the situation.

Summary

Behavior, not words, determines dominance. Good interviewers know that an air of confidence and ease typifies the behavior of truly dominant people; they are inclined to do as they please without asking permission and rarely offend others while doing so. On the other hand, arrogance and pomposity, characteristics often intended to pass for dominance, do not create dominance. They sometimes provide amusement, but more often than not, anger the people subjected to such behavior.

Suggested Reading

LaBordie, Genie Z. (1987). *Influencing with Integrity*. Palo Alto, CA: Syntony Publishing.

Morris, Desmond (1994). *Body Talk*. New York, NY: Crown Publishers, Inc.

Nierenberg, Gerald I. and Henry H. Calero (1971). *How to Read a Person Like a Book*. New York, NY: Hawthorne Books Inc.

Chapter 3
Essentials

Knowing the steps of an interview and understanding how to act when conducting an interview can go a long way toward helping a person become a competent interviewer. Unfortunately, this is only the starting point. Many other skills and techniques contribute to success in this field. Some of these apply so frequently as to merit regarding them as essentials.

Advice of Rights

In the well-known *Miranda* case, the court said only that law enforcement officers could not question a person in custody without first informing that person of the provisions of the Fifth Amendment to the United States Constitution, a seemingly innocuous requirement. However, few court decisions have had greater impact on police officers' behavior. It has caused many investigators to abandon all efforts to obtain confessions and has caused others to attempt to subvert the spirit, if not the letter, of the law. It has also prompted some administrators and lower courts to rule far on the cautious side in their interpretations of the decision. Their application of the ruling often seems to bear little resemblance to the intention of the Supreme Court. For example, one agency's policy requires its investigators to immediately seek out any person under investigation for suspected criminal activity and advise that person of his or her *Miranda* rights. Because of these problems, I will deal with *Miranda* in this section, which discusses the fundamentals of interviewing.

Due to various departmental policies and court rulings, investigators often find themselves required to give the *Miranda* warnings to many suspects and, occasionally, to witnesses. Investigators must comply and still avoid the "chilling effect" that this warning can produce. Those who succeed do so by regarding *Miranda* not as a hurdle to overcome, but as a tool for achieving their goal, the truth. For many, this may require purging themselves of preconceived notions about how to issue this warning.

Most good interrogators regard *Miranda* as a device to enhance the rapport-building process. If the suspect has no previous experience with arrest procedures, some interrogators use the *Miranda* warning as part of an overall explanation of what is in store for the suspect. They explain how the judicial process works and tell the suspect that the system intends to obtain the truth and dispose of the case based on that truth. When doing so, it will take into account the interests of both society and the suspect. The suspect therefore has everything to gain by providing his or her version of the matter. This approach makes sense, and therefore it works (sometimes).

Criminals with extensive records may be less inclined to accept this approach because they all have heard the following advice: "Don't say a word without your attorney present." One seasoned detective often deflated this attitude by introducing himself and immediately beginning the *Miranda* warning. When he arrived at the part that informs the suspect of his or her right to an attorney, he would pause, smile, and then interject the observation that of all the criminals waiting on death row, not one of them had gotten there without the benefit of an attorney. This type of statement may not completely eliminate the chilling effect of the *Miranda* warnings, but it certainly steers the conversation in a different direction.

> *Miranda* should imply, "I play fair; you can trust me."

Another investigator took advantage of suspects' many previous encounters with the law by suggesting that although he would like to hear their side of the story, he could not until he had advised them of their rights. The investigator would then feign some embarrassment at having to do this because he felt the suspects probably knew their rights better than most investigators. He would then say:

> You know, I feel silly sitting here reading this to you. There's no doubt in my mind that you know it at least as well as I do. Here's an idea, let's see if you can tell me everything this form says without even looking at it.

Most of them could and would do so without error. The investigator would then compliment them on their performance, review the form aloud to verify that they had "passed" the test and then ask the suspects if they had any objection to answering a few questions. A surprising number agreed to do so. Although this may sound a bit simplistic, it offers an alternative to the often-used approach, "You have the right to remain silent; I suggest you exercise that right."

The above examples illustrate how some investigators, without in any way violating either the letter or the spirit of the law, have converted a hurdle into a tool. *Miranda* need not, as some believe, end the procurement of lawful confessions.

Note-Taking

An investigator arrives at a door, introduces himself, states the reason for the visit, and receives an invitation to come inside. He begins by taking a notepad from his briefcase and asking the first question: "Are you Mrs. Johnson, and do you reside here at 123 Elm Street?" He then carefully writes the information on the pad while Mrs. Johnson waits.

Absent photographic memories or tape recorders, investigators must make note of the items they cannot remember and might later be called upon to recount. However, this presents a problem because note-taking interferes with conversation. It does this by causing extended pauses while the interviewer writes, and by reducing the interviewer's opportunity to observe the subject. Also, notepads and pencils inhibit people by reminding them that they may be held accountable for their words, thus prompting them to weigh them more carefully. Self-doubt will often prevent witnesses from furnishing information under the threat of having that information come back to haunt them. The pencil provides this threat.

Although notes may be essential, an interviewer should minimize note-taking. The investigator above had no need to record the name or address of Mrs. Johnson—he already knew it. Do not record what you already know because it will often prevent you from learning what you do not know.

> **A verbatim transcript has nothing in common with note-taking.**

Many effective interviewers resolve this dilemma by refraining from taking any notes until they reach the verification stage of the interview. They do not write during the questioning stage of the interview. Only when they are reviewing facts already obtained do they make any notes, and they limit these to the essentials needed to prompt their recall. This technique enables them to listen and watch more effectively during questioning and removes the inhibiting aspect of note-taking. By the time they begin writing, the person has already provided the information. The interviewers are merely ensuring that they have heard it correctly.

Listening

Many years ago, a flight instructor at the Pensacola, Florida Naval Air Station decided to document the claim of many of his associates that novice flight students do not listen to their instructors. The fledgling aviators always denied this accusation by pointing out that not only had they passed a stringent hearing test and wore earphones linked directly to the instructor, they verbally had to acknowledge every instruction given to them. These denials not withstanding, the instructor took a tape recorder with him on a training flight and turned it on as the flight began. The student, seated in front of the instructor, did not know about the recorder.

At the completion of the flight, as the instructor and the student walked back to the hanger, the instructor critiqued the student's efforts. He concluded with the question, "By the way, what did you think of the little gremlin who was with us today?" To this, the student responded, "What little gremlin?" The instructor told the student that along with the directions he had given the student throughout the flight, he had included a running saga of a little gremlin who first appeared on the port wing and proceeded to roam about the aircraft. Without the recording, the instructor could never have convinced the student that this had taken place. Not only did the student not question the instructor's account of the gremlin's activities, in response to the instructor's queries regarding the creature, the student had responded, "Aye, aye, sir!"

> **We listen with our brains more than with our ears.**

How could this happen? Because having good hearing and an effective intercom do not constitute *listening*. Listening, which is an active process, depends on mental involvement. The student, conditioned by previous flights, knew what the instructor was going to say and therefore had no reason to listen. Besides, he had problems of his own; he was trying to keep an airplane under control, a chore much higher on his list of priorities.

As a new instructor at the FBI Academy, I had the opportunity to observe a fellow instructor teach a course for which I would later have responsibility. On the first day of class, the instructor asked each member of the class to come to the front of the room and introduce him or herself. At the completion of this process, the instructor told the class the purpose of this exercise—to enable all members to get to know one another. He then named each member of the class.

This display of memory power amazed both the students and me. After the class, I asked him how he had managed to do that "trick." He said it was no trick, that he had merely listened to each student. I told him that I too had listened, and I could not have repeated one-half of the names, much less all of them. He replied:

> No, I mean I really listen and do not allow other thoughts to interfere. I concentrate totally on that person and the words spoken. At the completion of the introduction, the students have ceased to be just members of the class and have become individuals with faces and names.

When confronted with my own new class, I decided to try his technique. I, too, could and did name all 25 students. However, I hesitate to do this very often, not because of a fear of failure, but because of its effect on me—I felt as if I had run a marathon. It is exhausting. Total concentration for the 45 minutes consumes a great deal of energy. Listening is hard work, and we do it reluctantly unless the stakes are high. Unfortunately, unless we do it all of the time, we may miss a great deal.

Although concentration provides the key, many specific techniques can assist interviewers in enhancing their listening. These include:

- withholding judgment or at least not revealing any judgments prematurely

- providing nonverbal indicators of listening, such as nodding

- periodically paraphrasing what the speaker has said

Effective listening probably represents the single most important technique in the entire interview process. What is asked and what is said mean little; what is heard and understood means everything.

Summary

Many factors, some seemingly unrelated to the interview process, affect the quality and quantity of information obtained in an interview. Their effect usually depends more on the interviewers' attitudes than on their skills. Contrary to common opinion, an advice of rights can enhance rapport rather than curtail it, the average person can listen effectively if willing to commit the effort, and note-taking, if kept in perspective, need not hamper communication.

Suggested Reading

Gold, Susan Dudley (1995). *Miranda v. Arizona (1966)*. New York, NY: Henry and Company.

Knapp, Mark L. and Gerald R. Miller (eds.). (1994). *Handbook of Interpersonal Communication, 2nd edition*. Thousand Oaks, CA: Sage Publications.

Robertson, Arthur K. (1994). *Listen for Success*. Burr Ridge, IL: Irwin Professional Publishing.

Part II
Detecting Deception

Few experienced investigators will dispute the need to discern fact from fiction. Embarrassment and wasted time can result from believing lies told by either witnesses or suspects. Perhaps more important, interrogators obtain very few confessions unless they are absolutely convinced of the suspects' guilt. Absent strong evidence, interrogators can achieve this feeling of certainty only through the ability to recognize the difference between truth and deception.

Paul Ekman, noted author and researcher, conducted an experiment to learn how effectively law enforcement officers can detect deception. The experiment involved having an investigator face an individual who would either tell the truth or lie. This individual faced a projection screen on which various slides appeared periodically, and the person would then briefly describe what was on the screen or would provide a false description. The investigator, whose back was to the screen, then tried to determine if the person was lying.

Subsequently, an article appeared in a syndicated column announcing that members of various law enforcement agencies had done very poorly in this experiment. Only the Secret Service achieved even marginally better results than random guessing would have provided. The article concluded that law enforcement officers could not differentiate between truth and fiction—that they could not detect lies. However, it should have concluded that law enforcement officers could not detect deception under those particular circumstances, hardly the same thing.

Law enforcement officers can learn to detect deception, but many cannot do so under the conditions set up by Mr. Ekman. Instead, they must systematically apply detection techniques to a total interview process. Admittedly, some lack the patience to do it, and they rationalize this shortcoming by citing huge caseloads and insufficient time, an example of false economy. By discovering the truth as they go along, they would save time. They would need to interview fewer people and would have fewer false leads to check out.

Additionally, effective detection of deception can save enormous amounts of time by enabling the investigator to avoid going to court to testify: Solve a crime simply by developing reasonable evidence and a trial usually follows. Obtain a confession and often a trial never takes place.

Polygraphers, traditionally some of law enforcement's most successful inter-rogators, often hear the words, "The only reason you get so many confessions is because of your machine." Some machines may produce confessions, but the polygraph does not fit that category. The assumption that it can is annoying to polygraph examiners in several ways. First, they object to their device being called a machine—it is an instrument. Second, they insist that their instrument does not produce confessions—it merely confirms whether the suspect has told the truth. Once the examiner has confirmed whether the suspect is telling the truth, the instrument has no further role. The polygrapher then becomes an inter-rogator whose sole advantage over others comes from the confidence of know-ing the truth. Some investigators may regard this advantage as a luxury, but suc-cessful interrogators recognize it as a necessity.

Often, investigators can gain this same advantage enjoyed by the polygra-phers without benefit of their instrument. Although the polygraph may detect subtle physiological changes in liars that interviewers rarely hear or see, other, more obvious symptoms of deception often exist. The secret of success rests with the interrogator's ability to hear and see such symptoms and to recognize them as indicators of deception. Some investigators do this subconsciously, never knowing what they have seen or heard; they merely sense that a suspect has lied. As a result, their efforts to detect deception lack consistency, and they cannot explain the successes they do achieve. Training and practice can raise this "gut feeling" to a conscious level.

The following section will present some suggestions for detecting deception. Some will deal with the spoken word while others will emphasize nonverbal behavior. Although dealt with separately, in practice, interviewers must use these techniques simultaneously.

Chapter 4
Verbal Clues

"Listen kid," said the old-timer, "talk to any suspect long enough and sooner or later you'll catch him in a lie. When you do, you know you've got the right man." This advice usually results in attempts by interviewers to detect contradictions. Unfortunately, good liars rarely contradict themselves. Contradictions are only one verbal indicator of deception; investigators should listen for many others.

The Unimportant Flaw

Liars, when telling a story, must rely on their imagination; they have no actual memory of the event because it never happened. This lack of real experience from which to draw, coupled with concern for being caught in a lie, will often produce a story that varies in many ways from one recounted from memory. Not only will the facts differ, but the flavor of the story, the emphasis on various aspects, word selection, and omissions will also differ. By approaching the detection-of-deception process systematically, and looking and listening for these deviations from reality, investigators will increase their effectiveness. Not only will they "know" that the person has lied, they will know *why* they know. This gives the investigators a great deal of confidence and improves their chances of discovering the truth.

> **Telling one lie makes a person a liar so listen for little lies as well as big lies.**

When confronted by investigators, nearly all suspects, both the guilty and the innocent, will have prepared a version of the event in question. Usually they have had more than ample time to prepare and rehearse this story. Warren Holmes, a former Miami, Florida police officer and noted polygrapher and interrogator, stated in an FBI Academy lecture that investigators should listen to these stories very intently. He suggested that they should listen not just for the relevant facts but for the tangential items as well. In these areas, rather than when relating the critical parts, the guilty will often reveal themselves. They do so by making statements that Holmes says "fly in the face of reason."

Unlike the main issues, suspects often put little thought into these peripheral items. Instead, they regard them as mere filler, designed to make the transition from point to point. However, if these transitions contain a flaw, the suspect is lying. The old-timer was right, "Catch them in a lie and you know you have the right person." Mr. Holmes provided the following incident as an example of the seemingly unimportant fact that reveals the liar:

The story begins at an employees' parking lot at a major airport. A security officer, age 32, is on duty. At first glance, one could easily mistake him for a police officer; he has a uniform, badge, nightstick and handcuffs. He lacks only a gun and a radio. He has requested a radio but has not yet received it. Due to his seniority, he works the day shift, starting at 8:00 A.M. and ending at 4:00 P.M.

On the day in question, the officer's replacement arrives at 3:40 P.M. and suggests that because there is no need for both of them to remain, the officer might as well depart. The officer agrees, saying that he needs to get back to the office anyway. As he enters the office, he encounters his supervisor and a flight attendant. He and the flight attendant immediately recognize each other. She points at him and says, "That's the guy who assaulted me in the parking lot less than an hour ago. He responds, "That's the woman I just saw with the cocaine in the parking lot." The supervisor asks them to give their versions of what happened and the flight attendant relates the following:

> After returning from a flight, I got to my car shortly after 3:00 P.M. It was parked in an isolated part of the lot and I didn't see anybody around. I got into my car, started the engine and, because the air was a bit stuffy, I left the door open while I got a hairbrush from my purse and began to brush my hair. The next thing I knew, that guard was standing right beside me. I don't know where he came from or how long he had been there.

> He asked for my registration and parking permit that I keep in an envelope in the glove compartment. I had to lean over to my right to get it, and when I straightened up, he had put his right arm along the top of the front seat. As a result, he more or less had his arm draped just above my shoulders. This made me a bit nervous and uncomfortable, and I leaned forward while I fumbled through the envelope looking for the things he wanted.

> As I was doing this, he reached over with his left hand and put it on my thigh. I don't know what reaction he expected, but it must not have been the one he got. I let out a scream, sat upright, and turned toward him all at one time. He seemed startled and immediately stepped back about three steps. I reached over, grabbed the door, slammed it shut, put the car in gear and took off. I was quite shaken, and all I wanted to do was get away from that guy.

As I got close to the airport exit, which took about 15 minutes, I began to realize that I couldn't just run away. I couldn't let him get away with what he had done. Besides, I would have to park there again and who knows what he might do the next time.

At that point, I turned around and came back here to report him, and that's the guy who did it.

The supervisor says that he understands and then nods to the security officer. The security officer, having listened to the flight attendant's story, responds with his version:

Part of her story is correct; her car was parked in an isolated area of the lot; she did get in, start the engine and leave the door open. It was a nice day, and I was wandering around the lot and saw her do it. I was standing about 30 feet back from her at an angle, and she didn't see me.

However, when she got in the car, it was not a hair brush she took from her purse; it was a clear plastic bag with a white powder in it. Now I might not be a detective, but I knew what I was looking at. I then started to walk toward the car, and when I got within about 10 feet of it, something must have alerted her to my presence. Either she caught sight of me in the mirror, saw a shadow or something. She looked around at me, slammed the door and took off. I didn't get her license plate, but I had enough of a description of her and the car that I could have notified the guard at the main gate if I had had a radio. Because I don't, and because I have been told not to leave my area except in matters of life and death, I had to wait for my relief to arrive so I could come back here to report the incident.

Fortunately, he came about 20 minutes early. I told him I needed to get back to the office right away and came here as quickly as I could. However, in this case I guess it doesn't matter because that's the woman I saw!

Should the supervisor believe the flight attendant or the security officer? Trying to decide, he may go over each version, looking for flaws or contradictions. He might ask himself, "Why would the flight attendant come back if she were guilty? Why would she take drugs from her purse in a location where she might be seen? Why didn't the security officer leave his post to report the incident? Why didn't he move to the car more quickly?" Unfortunately, dissecting the two stories might show poor judgment on the part of both participants, but it will not reveal the liar. In real life, people do not always do the reasonable thing, but this does not necessarily make them villains.

To solve this problem, the supervisor should look beyond the respective accounts of what happened at the scene. The secret lays in understanding the nature of the parking lot security officer. With few exceptions, he has all the trappings of a police officer, and in his own mind he probably regards himself as one. When he looks in the mirror, he sees a cop. Yet in the years he has been working there, probably the most exciting "case" that he investigated involved an illegally parked vehicle. This mundane job conflicts with his self-image.

Now an incident worthy of his image has taken place. This case has the makings of a television show. The crime, drug possession, is in vogue; the female flight attendant provides some allure; flight from the scene adds some drama. At last he has some action. Yet when his relief arrived, the officer did not tell him of the event. This would almost never happen. He would have greeted his relief with the words, "You aren't going to believe what just happened!" For him to do otherwise almost defies belief. If he did not tell the story to the first person he met, particularly a co-worker with similar interests, the event probably did not happen.

Listening provides the key. Listen to what is said and how it is said. Also, listen for what is not said. If the suspect lies about even one part of the story, that makes the suspect a liar.

A Change in Demeanor

Suppose that, after listening to a suspect's account, you can detect no such flaw. Tell the suspect you would like to go over the story again. However, this time, as the suspect tells the story, interrupt at various points and ask for additional details. For instance, suppose a suspect claims to have witnessed a street crime from the third-story window of a department store and therefore could not have committed the crime. Ask the suspect for details regarding the window. Was it decorated? Was the glass clear or tinted? What had the suspect been doing just before he looked out the window?

These types of questions have two essential characteristics: they relate to what the subject has said but, at the same time, offer little chance that the suspect will have anticipated them. The first characteristic makes the questions reasonable, and the second requires answers that the suspect will not have rehearsed. These questions will not affect the truthful person. However, they will cause difficulty for the liar. The liar must concern him or herself with the purpose of each question and how best to answer it.

Listen carefully for the suspect's tone and demeanor as he or she responds. The actual answer takes second place to the delivery of the answer. More to the point, listen for a change in delivery.

> **Unexpected questions irritate liars,
> and they show it.**

Most guilty people who have consented to an interview do so with the intention of convincing the interviewer of their innocence. They thus feel compelled to feign a sincere desire to cooperate and get to the truth. This calm and often ingratiating behavior will usually disappear during this elaboration phase of the interview. Responses such as, "What's that got to do with anything?" and, "How much longer is this going to take?" are not uncommon, although just a few minutes prior the suspect showed nothing but cooperation. *A significant change in demeanor or attitude when confronted with unanticipated but relevant questions usually indicates deception.* This change results from the discomfort the liar feels when he or she is forced to fabricate answers on the spur of the moment.

The Trap

Most good traps use an appealing lure. For fishing, a lure may resemble an injured minnow, and in a chess match, a lure may consist of a seemingly careless sacrifice of a piece. In interviewing, it may be the interviewer conveying the feeling that he believes the suspect. This feeling may encourage the suspect to commit to a detailed account of his actions during a critical period. Once the suspect makes such a commitment, the interviewer can spring the trap:

> Now, don't get me wrong, I'm not saying you killed that guy. What I'm asking is, when the boys from the lab are finished processing the alley where the crime took place, is it possible they might find some indication that you had been there? As you know, with DNA technology, they can pick up even the slightest trace of human presence, and they will compare it with everybody even remotely suspected, and that has to include you because you are known to have been in the vicinity. Any chance at all they will find some indication that you had been there in the past few days? Just there, not that you did anything wrong.

Imagine the dilemma the above question poses for the guilty suspect who has already denied ever having been in the alley. If a suspect changes a story because of such a question, the investigator should regard the suspect as untruthful. The suspect felt the need to change the story to fit a new set of facts. A truthful person would not do this.

An effective trap question should meet several criteria: It should not be accusatory; it should be based on potential evidence currently under development; and it should be asked only after the suspect has committed to a statement that the evidence might refute. In answer to the question regarding the alley, the innocent suspect will continue to deny having been there, but the guilty will often change their story and provide an outlandish scenario to account for the potential contradiction:

> As I told you, I've never been in that alley, but, come to think of it . . .

A guilty person will change his or her story to fit the evidence.

What comes after this is irrelevant; "come to think of it" is the flag; the suspect *has* been in the alley and *has* lied about it. The rest of the story follows:

> . . . come to think of it, a couple of days ago I was on the park bench about a block down from there when I got this urge for a beer. There's a deli there, and I bought a quart of beer and sat on the bench and drank it out of the bottle that I kept in the paper bag. I didn't want the whole quart, but they didn't sell regular bottles.
>
> I drank about half of it and was debating what to do with the rest. I thought about pouring it out when I noticed this bum sitting about two benches down who was watching me really closely. It was obvious he wanted that beer, so I left it on the bench, got up and left.
>
> Now I'm not saying this happened, but that bum certainly got the rest of that beer, and he may have taken that bottle into the alley. Other than that, there is no way you're gonna find anything to show I was ever in that alley.

A variation on this technique can be used to evaluate an alibi, particularly when the suspect claims to have been somewhere else, alone:

> You said the robbery took place over on the east side of town at 8:00? Well, that rules me out. I was at the Biograph Theater over on the west side. I saw *Gone with the Wind*; it started at 7:00 and wasn't over until after 10:00.

The subject has committed himself to a specific location at a specific time. Now the investigator can fabricate an event to determine whether the alibi is true:

> The Biograph? That's right down the street from where that garbage truck hit a pole and knocked out a transformer about 9:30. Traffic lights were out until after 11:00, and traffic was a real mess. How long did it take you to get out of there?

Again, if the suspect attended the movie, he will react spontaneously. He may be astonished by the statement, but he will not have to hesitate while he ponders how to respond. The lying subject, however has a real dilemma. He has no idea how to react. If he agrees that the traffic was terrible and no accident occurred, he loses. Conversely, if it did happen and he denies a problem, he loses. Listen not only for the answer but for the spontaneity of the response. Only the most accomplished liars can take this in stride.

Use of similar ploys has occasionally resulted in a confession. The suspect, convinced of the damning evidence against him, surrenders. Usually these come from the unintelligent, but they can also come from the naive:

Joe, take a look at this photo taken by the surveillance camera. The guy must be pretty sure that nobody can recognize him with those coveralls and ski mask. He is certainly in for a rude awakening. As you know, through the use of laser technology, they can remove one layer of light-sensitive material at a time. The boys in the lab are doing that right now. Now once they have removed the mask from this photo, whose face is going to be there, Joe? It's going to be yours, isn't it, Joe?

As ridiculous as it may seem, this and similar ruses sometimes succeed. They succeed because, stated with confidence, they convince the suspect that irrefutable evidence will arrive momentarily. With some, this produces a confession. Regardless, if tailored to the capacity and mental state of the suspect, they will often produce reactions that provide investigators with the assurance that they have the correct suspect.

Indicator Questions

Interrogators have noted that, despite the creativity of many liars, they often behave in predictable ways, particularly regarding how they answer certain questions. Their goals, escape and evasion, channel them into paths of predictable behavior. Innocent people answer truthfully without concern for how the interviewer might interpret them. The guilty weigh each answer for its effect. Many of them often reach similar conclusions and therefore answer many questions in a predictable, self-serving way. While no single response signifies guilt, a pattern of answers may.

As indicated earlier, interviewers usually introduce themselves by giving their name, position, and purpose. However, many interviewers have found that when confronting suspects, asking them if they know why they are being interviewed often provides some insight. For instance, a detective investigating an internal theft at a business may decide to interview each employee who had access to the missing items. "Do you know why I want to talk to you?" may be the first question asked of each suspect. The innocent person will almost always know why because the company grapevine will have taken care of that. However, the guilty person is not nearly so well-informed. To acknowledge knowing the reason requires him or her to admit knowing about the crime. Guilty people will often choose to remain as far from that as possible despite the unreasonableness of their response. For the same reason, they rarely will have discussed the matter with family or friends and, even if they have, they will usually deny having done so.

> **Criminals rarely know that a crime took place.**

Another question that innocent people readily answer that causes problems for the guilty calls for speculation:

> You've worked here for several years and have gotten to know many
> of the employees pretty well. In your opinion, who is the person least
> likely to be involved in something like this?

Every company has some employees who are well-known for their honesty, and investigators should note a suspect's failure to identify them. Such information reduces the number of viable suspects, and guilty people do not like this. They often attempt to enlarge the field of suspects by a response such as the following:

> I guess it could have been anyone who works here. In fact, security is
> pretty lax around here; it just as easily could have been somebody
> from outside.

The list of suspects just increased dramatically.

Although interviewers can do it, getting people to speculate regarding possible culprits requires some effort. People try to avoid being labeled as rats or snitches. Interviewers might handle this by saying:

> I'm not asking you to finger anybody, and this is just between you and
> me. If you were working this case and had to list the suspects in order
> of most to least likely, who would you list first?

Contrary to what many might expect, the guilty rarely point the finger at someone else. Innocent people will usually speculate once the stigma of snitch or rat has been removed. The guilty usually do not want to speculate. They do not have to because they know who did it.

When asked to comment on the nature of the culprit who would commit such a crime, the guilty tend to show more understanding than the innocent. To take advantage of this inclination, an interviewer might say:

> This theft has caused a lot of problems for the company and many of
> its employees. What kind of person would do something like this, and
> what should happen to that person when we solve this?

Even for the innocent, being interviewed as a potential suspect produces concern and discomfort, and these feelings rarely result in sympathy for the culprit. Thus, responses that minimize the nature of the punishment or offer justification for the crime rarely come from those who are innocent. Only the guilty have such charitable inclinations. Note the absence of any mention of criminal motive or jail. The guilty do not speak in such harsh terms about themselves:

> Somebody would really have to be desperate to do this.

> I'd say they are probably sick and need some help.

I think they certainly should have to pay the money back.

They probably should be fired.

There's no way they should be trusted with money anymore.

Although we usually admire compassionate people, sometimes the compassion loses its charm and takes on a different aura. The above responses are nothing more than veiled self-serving pleas for leniency.

Successful liars often try to stay as close to the truth as they can because they realize that this tactic makes them less vulnerable to detection. A question that seemingly allows them to exercise this ploy could be worded in the following manner:

> Now, I'm not saying you did this, but have you ever seriously thought
> about how you could do something like this and get away with it? I
> don't mean just a passing idea, but really thought through how you
> could do it?

For the guilty, the truthful answer obviously is, "Yes." Remarkably, they will often admit to having considered doing the crime but will follow this with a denial of the act. They do this because they cannot be held responsible for what they think and therefore can make this admission and even elaborate on it with impunity. They need only tack on a minor lie, a sort of afterthought, "But I wouldn't do it."

Question:	**Did you ever seriously think about doing this?**
Guilty:	**Sure, but I would never do it.**
Innocent:	**No, of course not.**

More importantly, they believe that the "correct" answer is "Yes." They regard themselves as normal and thus assume that everybody thinks that way. However, they are wrong because honest people do not go around thinking about how to steal things. Interestingly—and something to remember—many people in law enforcement also come to regard this thought process as normal. Take for example, a secretary, married to a veteran police officer, who discovered that the diamond in her engagement ring had fallen from its setting. A thorough search of the entire office failed to locate it. She also searched her car and her home without success. Upon arrival at work the next day, she found on her desk a 3 x 5 card with the diamond taped to it. The card also had a note from the cleaning lady indicating that she had found it. The secretary telephoned the cleaning lady

and learned that she had found it by her desk. She thanked her and then regarded the incident as closed.

When she told her husband about this, he couldn't believe it. It amazed him
that this woman had found a valuable, unidentifiable diamond and had not kept
it. He suggested his wife buy the woman flowers, take her to lunch, and give her
a reward. His wife could not understand. Why should she do all of this? After
all, the only thing the woman had done was to return some property to its owner,
a normal act for an honest person. For different reasons, crooks and cops have
difficulty understanding this.

By weaving leading questions into the interview and keeping track of the
answers, interviewers can determine whether a deceitful pattern exists. Noting a
preponderance of answers whose purpose seems intended to mitigate or exoner-
ate rather than to inform provides the key. This recognition can raise an intuitive
feeling about possible deception to a conscious level of understanding.

Attempts to Convince

"Believe me when I'm telling you; I swear this on my mother's grave and my
children's eyes." These words prefaced every fabrication furnished by a former
informant of mine. Like most good informants, he would often perceive what we
wanted to know and, if unable to develop the information, would offer speculation and rumor as if it were fact. Never when he had firm information did he use
this preface because he felt no need to do so.

Question:	**"Are you telling the truth?"**
Answer:	**"Lying does not come easy to me."**

If interviewers reduce the initial anxiety caused by their presence, and
refrain from making accusations, few innocent people will feel the need to convince the interviewers of their honesty. They let the facts speak for themselves.
Only the guilty feel compelled to profess their innocence; they cannot rely on
the facts. They also often provide far more information than is requested of them
in hopes of convincing the interviewer of their innocence.

In response to the question: "Did you rob the liquor store?" an innocent suspect is apt to respond, "No!" The actual robber might give an assortment of reasons why he could not have done such a thing:

"I'm not a thief."

"Why would I do that? I have plenty of money."

"I wasn't raised that way."

Not only do these responses provide unsolicited information, none of them answers the question, a ploy that is common among liars.

Summary

Truthful people recount events from memory; thus, their stories sound real. Liars must use their imagination and, even when given plenty of time to prepare, their stories often have a hollow ring that can be heard by the attentive interviewer. In addition, because the guilty comment about themselves and their own actions, they often sprinkle self-serving, mitigating terms throughout their accounts. If not forthcoming on their own, interviewers can often prompt the guilty to provide these indicators by asking leading questions that will have no effect on the innocent.

Suggested Reading

Inbau, Fred E. and John E. Reid (1986). *Criminal Interrogations and Confessions*. Baltimore, MD: William and Wilkins.

Lewis, Michael and Carolyn Saarni (eds.). (1993). *Lying and Deception in Everyday Life*. New York, NY: The Guilford Press.

Rudacille, Wendell C. (1994). *Identifying Lies in Disguise*. Dubuque, IA: Kendall Hunt Publishing Co.

Chapter 5
Nonverbal Clues

Predators devoured neither your cave-dwelling ancestors nor mine, at least not until after our ancestors had reproduced. Predators killed many prehistoric people, but why not our ancestors? Because our ancestors knew how to get away. The natural selection process refined this ability over hundreds of thousands of years, and our ancestors passed it on to us.

The Fight-or-Flight Response

Have you seen any saber-toothed tigers lately? If so, your system would react in much the same way that your ancestors' systems did. They have passed to you the reflex response known as *fight-or-flight*. This phenomenon evolved to enhance the body functions needed for survival during a crisis, while muting many irrelevant ones. These include:

- Adrenalin and sugar are released into the bloodstream.

- Pulse and breathing rates increase.

- Sweat glands activate.

- Pupils dilate.

- Salivary glands shut down.

- Digestion ceases.

Investigators, when they encounter a guilty person, represent the modern version of the saber-toothed tiger. They pose a threat, and this threat produces the effects developed through evolution. Internally, the suspect's body prepares to run or fight. However, outwardly the guilty person must mask these responses. He or she cannot run, fight, or even show any indication of wanting to do so. This conflict produces its own set of symptoms that, if observed, can provide much insight for the investigator.

Almost anybody will display some signs of anxiety when interviewed by a law enforcement agent. This makes the rapport-building process vital because building rapport reduces this initial anxiety. Interviewers can even put the guilty person at ease to some extent by convincing him or her that they pose no immediate threat. Once they develop rapport, interviewers can determine an interviewee's truthful behavior through observation while discussing routine, nonthreatening matters. Interviewers must do this because they will need it for comparison when they reach the critical points of the interview where the guilty person must lie.

Guilt leaks through even the best mask.

Researchers have conducted many studies and written volumes regarding the specific actions that reveal deception. Nervous mannerisms, grooming gestures, shifting of postures, and yawning are only a few of the signals that show anxiety. All of them result from the suspect's attempts to mask stress. Regardless of the suspect's efforts to appear unconcerned, some of these subtle stress indicators will usually filter through.

Changes in behavior mean more than the behavior itself.

However, interviewers need not commit to memory a long list of deceptive behaviors. In fact, some investigators suggest that just as statistics do not apply to an individual, neither do behaviors such as nervous movements, sweating, and poor eye contact necessarily show deception by all who display them. They merely serve as guidelines. How, then, can interviewers use nonverbal behavior fostered by the flight-or-fight response to detect deception? They can do so by following this simple step-by-step procedure:

- Build rapport.

- Learn the suspect's truthful behavior.

- Look for deviations from truthful behavior when the discussion turns to relevant matters.

- Withhold judgment until certain that the timing of these changes coincides with the shift to relevant topics.

- Ensure that these behaviors occur each time relevant topics are discussed; do not base your decision on a single occurrence.

Creativity (Neuro-Linguistic Programming)

As previously noted, when Bandler and Grinder observed the relationship between eye movements and modes of thought, they were concerned with rapport-building capabilities. Although they also noted that a person could distinguish between recall and creativity by observing these movements, they placed little emphasis on this capability. They observed that when people used the creative portion of their brains, their eye movements tended to show mirror images of the movements exhibited when they searched their memories. Thus, people who looked up and left when recalling an actual event would look up and right when creating one. Other modes performed similarly. Therefore, after interviewers learn a person's normal recall eye patterns, they can then look for deviations from these patterns for indicators of creativity.

> **Shifting eye patterns equal shifty-eyed.**

Creativity plays an essential role in the world of art and entertainment. In the world of interviewing, creativity on the part of a suspect takes on a more sinister aura; it is called lying. Interviewers can readily use suspects' eye movements to detect deception. Just as with any other nonverbal behavior, before using it for detecting deception, interviewers must determine the truthful behavior of their suspects. They can do this by observing the suspects' eye movements while asking routine, nonthreatening questions that require suspects to search their memories. Once they have done this, interviewers need only look for deviations from these patterns when they ask relevant questions. These deviations suggest an attempt to create—to lie.

Summary

The polygraph can detect changes in the body that result from the anxiety of being caught in a lie; interviewers can also observe some of these changes. "Change" is the key word. The interviewer must first note the suspects' behaviors when they are telling the truth. These actions can include body and eye movement, breathing rate and depth, nervous mannerisms, and any other observable actions or patterns of behavior. The interviewer can then compare these with the behaviors displayed when asking potentially incriminating questions. Consistent deviations from known truthful behavior strongly suggest deception.

Suggested Reading

Burgoon, Judee K., David B. Buller and W. Gill Woodall (1994). *Nonverbal Communication*. Columbus, OH: Greyden Press.

Ekman, Paul (1984). *Unmasking the Face*. Palo Alto, CA: Consulting Psychologists Press.

Knapp, Mark L. and Judith A. Hall (1992). *Nonverbal Communication in Human Reaction*. Orlando, FL: Harcourt Brace Jovanovich Publishers.

Chapter 6
Statement Analysis

"I'm telling you," said Joe Blow, "Joe Blow is an honest man." Honest people rarely will talk about themselves in the third person, but con artists often do. Scrutiny of this tendency reveals its self-serving nature. It is often an attempt to provide a personal testimonial. However, in the normal flow of an interview, this and many other verbal indicators of deceit may go undetected.

As a result, some investigators advocate having the suspect's statements reduced to writing. This method is championed by Avinoam Sapir using a process that he calls *scientific content analysis*. This technique stresses the need to obtain the suspect's own words, untainted by clues from the investigator. Suspects may either write their statements themselves or dictate them to the investigator. Once investigators have obtained the suspect's written statement, they can analyze it at leisure.

Pronouns

Of all the areas open to examination in a written statement that might go unheard in an interview, pronoun usage, because it is universal, seems to offer the greatest opportunity for providing insight into a suspect's thinking. The absence of pronoun usage also can provide insight into a suspect's thoughts:

> I got up. I took a shower. I ate breakfast, and then I went to work. Arrived at work. Began the new project. Worked on it until 1:00 and then ate lunch.

The absence of "I" in the latter portion of that statement suggests an unwillingness to show involvement by the person providing the information; it is extremely impersonal. It becomes particularly telling when contrasted with the initial portion of the statement that does contain commitments. The investigator now must decide why this change occurred. Did something happen during the morning at work? Is there a problem with the new project? Why did the suspect show a reluctance to acknowledge any personal involvement during this time? The answers to these questions may solve a mystery. They certainly provide an area for additional conversation.

Most people, when asked to recount a past event in which they participated, will tell the story using the pronoun *I*, if alone, or *we*, if others also took part. Either is acceptable and does not suggest a problem. A change in usage, however, particularly if the change is from "I" to "we," should catch the investigator's attention. This often suggests an attempt by those seeking to dilute their own culpability by implying the involvement of others—this spreads the blame. A shift to the plural in a statement that began in the singular should alert the investigators and prompt them to carefully examine the portion of the statement where the change occurs.

Not only can a change from singular to plural dilute responsibility, people can further distance themselves from culpability by changing to third-person usage or even switching to the impersonal or passive. Consider the implications of the following statements made by a company representative. With each succeeding statement, the representative moves further away from personal responsibility:

> I always lock the safe.
>
> We always lock the safe.
>
> They always lock the safe.
>
> The safe is always locked.

Pronoun usage and position can also provide insight into relationships:

> We visited our kids.
>
> My wife and I visited our kids.
>
> I visited our kids with my wife.
>
> I visited the kids with the wife.

Note the gradual separation between the husband and his wife and finally the absence of the possessives *our* and *my*. On the other hand, the use of indicators of closeness by a victim when describing an encounter with an assailant should also raise suspicion.

Which victim was abducted?
Victim #1:   Then he took me into the woods.
Victim #2:   Then we went into the woods.

Verb Tense

When recounting a past event, people usually use the past tense. The event has already taken place, and to tell about it in the present tense makes no sense. With few exceptions, investigators would do well to take note of any past event discussed in the present tense. Consider the following statement made by an employee regarding her morning activities:

> I got up early and went to work. It was early when I arrived and nobody was there. I go directly to my desk and begin working. I was at my desk when the rest of the staff came in.

Truth or Lie? *"I pick up the gun and it goes off."*

When remembering, the mind sees what has occurred. However, if no memory of an event exists, the mind must create the occurrence as it goes along. Thus, people often tell a fabricated event as if it were taking place at that time. Investigators should pay particular attention to instances in which statements begin in the past and switch to the present. In these cases, experience has shown that the portion in the present tense almost always contains some degree of deception. The narrators are usually relating what they think should have happened. In the above example, there is reason to question whether she went directly to her desk and began working. If she did not, what did she do?

Editing

Most of us have learned to edit our thoughts before speaking, and our associates appreciate this. Nobody wants to hear a medical history report in response to the question, "How are you?" The same editing process occurs when a person writes an account of an event, and often clues will be present that will reveal this process. These clues are usually unnecessary phrases that the person substitutes for the missing information. Looking for these editing phrases can provide some insight:

> Saturday morning I cut the grass. After I cut the grass, I put the mower away.

Did the person believe that without the introduction, "After I cut the grass," we might think he put the mower away while cutting the grass? If not, why did he say it? Probably because he did many other mundane tasks he did not wish to bore us with and therefore chose to edit them out of the statement. Unnecessary phrases that suggest editing may have more sinister meaning when provided by a crime suspect and can serve as beacons that should alert the investigator to deliberate omissions. Examine the following:

> I walked into the room and saw him lying on the floor. I checked to see if he was breathing; he wasn't. After I checked for breathing, I ran to the phone and called the police.

What occurred between the checking of the body and the calling of the police? Was something sinister or something merely foolish done? The phrase, "After I checked for breathing," suggests that the person has omitted something. The investigator now has an additional area to probe and can do so with some confidence that at least something else did occur. Exhibiting such confidence during an interview may convince the interviewee to divulge the truth—it certainly will help.

Balance

Look for balance in a person's account of an event. Stories have an introduction, a body, and a conclusion. The body should deal with the significant issue and should make up most of the story. Beware of the alleged robbery victim who takes two pages to tell about getting dressed, having breakfast, and checking out of the motel and then in three sentences recounts the robbery that happened to him as he went to his car. This is akin to the ill-prepared student who feels compelled to fill the blank pages of a test booklet. Lacking sufficient relevant facts, the student may include much information that has little to do with the topic of the exam.

Nearly everyone appreciates succinctness by storytellers. However, a suspect who reduces an important and traumatic event to three sentences, particularly if that same person just spent two pages relating preliminary trivia, should raise serious questions. Keeping the critical event succinct also reduces the amount of time spent on it and therefore reduces the chance of making a mistake.

> **What's missing in this story?**
> **"Once upon a time, the prince and**
> **the princess lived happily ever after."**

How the suspect ends the story can also provide some insight. After a lengthy introduction and a succinct body, the suspect may give another long account of items that pose no threat. Liars will occasionally feel so relieved to have gotten through the critical phase that this relief manifests itself in a subsequent rambling account of meaningless details.

Usually, however, this does not happen. Investigators note that many liars, having postponed the lie and finally having gotten it out, feel free to stop. Their stories often lack a reasonable conclusion, particularly considering the lengthy introduction. Recounted events should sound as though they actually occurred. The lack of balance in an account can detract from this. Investigators often say, "I can't put my finger on it, but there's something wrong with his story." When analyzing a written statement, look for balance. A lack of balance may be the cause of the feeling that there is something wrong with a person's story.

Extraneous Information

A detective, trying to decide whether he is dealing with a suspect or a witness, said: "Tell me what happened."

> Well, I was just walking along when I saw this guy with a knife run by me. I have been walking along here for years and never saw anything like this. My office is just two blocks over and I often cut through this alley. It saves me about 10 minutes. My boss is a real stickler for punctuality, and so I pay attention to such things. I'm within a few years of retirement and . . .

The detective's request for an account of what happened has gone mostly unheeded. After the first sentence, everything provided is an explanation for the individual's presence, not what happened.

> **Hearing how to build a watch does not tell us the time.**

A common deceptive maneuver involves providing a small amount of relevant information and then interminably explaining that information. The devious try to dupe others into believing that quantity equals quality, and some do it very well. Their stories flow so smoothly that they often convince their listeners that their stories are complete. Having a written account to review can prevent this subterfuge from working by making these irrelevant explanations more apparent. Investigators can look at each portion of a statement and ask themselves, "Does this tell what happened, or does it tell why something happened?" Those that tell "why" often represent attempts to justify or mislead.

Possession of a written account in the suspect's own words provides the investigator with the opportunity to review it for all of the above indicators, and the process has proven quite effective. Despite this, many investigators, either because they regard the taking of a written statement as too time-consuming or because they feel that a suspect is incapable of furnishing a coherent statement, dismiss the idea of applying statement analysis in their cases.

However, even investigators who view statement taking as impractical in their circumstances should not dismiss the statement analysis process because attentive investigators can often hear indicators as they conduct an interview.

Summary

A story contains more than just facts; *how* a person says something may reveal far more. Reducing a person's statement to a verbatim transcript provides investigators with the opportunity to examine a statement thoroughly, and this often gives them insight beyond what the person intended to convey. Pronouns can show the nature of relationships; extraneous information often reveals efforts to justify or mislead; editing phrases provides clues to missing information; present tense verbs imply fabrication; and an unbalanced statement lacks credibility. Armed with this insight, the interviewer has a much better chance of obtaining the truth during the subsequent interview.

Suggested Reading

Rabon, Don (1994). *Investigative Discourse Analysis*. Durham, NC: Carolina Academic Press.

Weintraub, Walter (1989). *Verbal Behavior in Everyday Life*. New York, NY: Springfield Publishing Company.

Part III
Interrogation

A rape suspect, arrested the previous evening, sits in front of a desk located in an interview room of a police station. A detective seated behind the desk informs the suspect of the charge against him, advises him of his rights, and obtains background information. The following exchange then takes place:

> **Cross-examinations don't get confessions.**

Officer: I've talked to the arresting officers, and there is no reason for you to prolong this. You might as well tell me the whole story and make it easy on yourself.

Suspect: There's no way I could have raped that woman. I was at home at 10:00 watching TV; I didn't even leave the house until 11:00.

Officer: I hope for your sake that you can do better than that. You got anybody who can verify that?

Suspect: No, I don't; I was home alone. That's not a crime, you know.

Officer: So you were watching TV at 10:00? How convenient. You know that's the time the rape occurred. What show were you watching?

Suspect: I don't remember. I kinda fell asleep. Some old movie, I think.

Officer: Yeah, sure. You don't have cable, and there weren't any movies on the local stations at that time. I know because I checked. So much for your alibi, now tell me the truth.

Suspect: I'm telling you I was home alone; I didn't rape anybody.

Officer:	You were picked up in the vicinity within an hour of the rape. You fit the description given by the victim. You've been convicted of public lewdness in the past. You've contradicted yourself numerous times here today, and your alibi has more holes in it than a sieve. Now, why don't you give it up? Just admit it. You raped her, didn't you?
Suspect:	I didn't rape the woman.
Officer:	Don't lie to me; I know you did it.
Suspect:	No I didn't.
Officer:	The hell you didn't!
Suspect:	The hell I did!
Officer:	Hey Charlie, come get this guy and lock him up. I'm sick of wasting my time. He's never gonna talk.

Investigators who bombard suspects with a series of questions often believe that they have conducted an interrogation; after all, detectives do it that way in the movies. Instead, they have conducted a cross-examination, and no matter how well done, confessions rarely result. Cross-examinations are intended to discredit interviewees, not produce confessions. In the presence of juries, they might help to obtain convictions by making suspects look guilty, but they do not make suspects confess. Only lawyers on television obtain confessions in the courtroom, and even they obtain them from the gallery, not the witness stand.

"Do you want to buy a car?" Any car salesperson who relies on this approach should have another source of income. People do not buy cars because a sales representative asks them if they want to buy a car.

"Did you rob the bank?" Likewise, investigators who use this approach to obtain confessions should gather a great deal of evidence for trial because they will obtain few, if any, confessions. Questions do not produce confessions any more than they sell cars. Despite this, many, if not most investigators, continue to rely on questions as their technique for obtaining admissions. Most recognize that a simple, "Did you do it?" will not suffice, so instead they rely on a series of questions designed to discredit the suspects. Having shown that their suspects are liars, they assume that logic and common sense will lead the culprits to acknowledge the futility of further resistance. At this point they expect the guilty to confess. Few do.

People buy cars because salespeople give them good reasons to do so, and criminals confess because investigators do likewise. They offer the guilty person some acceptable reasons to tell the truth. Absent sufficient evidence, only this technique offers a reasonable chance of producing a conviction.

Chapter 7
Structure of an Interrogation

As we have seen, despite the uniqueness of each interview, most follow a general format or structure, and so do interrogations. Although terminology may vary depending on the course taken or the text read, most successful interrogators advocate many of the same basic principles and techniques.

Phase One: Make the Accusation

After reviewing all of the facts and conducting a thorough interview of the suspect, the detective concluded that, despite the suspect's claim that he had never met the victim, he had the right person. He had also used the interview to enhance his understanding of the suspect's motivations and values. He then said to the subject:

> Joe, based on what I already knew plus what I've learned from talking with you, there is no doubt that you are not being completely candid with me. You are the person who was with that woman last night, and she claims that you raped her. What we have to do now is get beyond the fact that you did it. There are two sides to every story, and all we have right now is one side. We need to get your version so we can get the truth working for you rather than against you.

Without this accusation or some variation of it, the actual interrogation never really begins. However, many investigators find this difficult to do. Rather than do so, they will dance around the topic of culpability and discuss in general, nonaccusatory terms, the need to get to the truth. This approach rarely has an effect on the guilty. It calls for no real denial because it fails to affix blame, and it thus enables the suspect to ignore the issue.

Even those who wish to confess rarely do so unless confronted with their guilt because human nature resists doing something unpleasant if other options exist. Absent a firm accusation, suspects will continue to hope for one of those options to appear. Interrogators must destroy these hopes as a first step to obtaining a confession.

> **The suspect must know that you know he or she is guilty.**

Not only does the accusation clearly change the process to an adversarial one by removing any doubt in the suspect's mind of the interrogator's opinion, it also offers a last opportunity for the interrogator to assess the suspect's guilt. Although interrogators should not make such allegations until they feel quite certain that they have the correct suspect, this accusation can do much to eliminate any lingering doubts.

Only one reaction to such an accusation suggests innocence—an immediate and firm denial often accompanied by anger. Consider your reaction if someone asked you if you knew what happened to the money missing from his desk. If after you said, "No," he then said he knew you took it—how long would it take you to respond to him? How long would it take you to become angry? Not long at all. Many experienced interrogators recommend making the accusation while standing beyond arms' reach. Accuse an innocent person and you may receive a violent reaction. Fortunately, guilty people rarely respond in such a fashion, and often they do not react at all. Initially, they just sit there as if they heard nothing.

> | Interviewer: | I know you did it. |
> |---|---|
> | Guilty: | Who, me? |
> | Innocent: | Like hell I did! |

Usually even the guilty finally will react, but their reactions lack spontaneity; they will delay. They often use this delay to change postures, cross arms and legs, and otherwise feign what they regard as indicators of righteous indignation. No matter how impressive a subsequent denial may sound, the investigator should consider this lack of spontaneity as a strong sign of guilt.

Many suspects will attempt to disguise their guilt by feigning incredulity and saying they simply cannot believe the interrogator would make such an allegation. "Are you telling me you think I did it?" or "Are you talking to me?" or "Who, me?" These are unnecessary questions in response to the statement: "There's no doubt in my mind that you did it." Also, note that none of these responses is a denial.

Phase Two: Present a Sales Pitch

From this point on, interrogators should tolerate no further discussion. They should immediately cut off any comments or defenses offered by the suspect. The interrogator might proceed:

> What we need to do now is get beyond the fact that you did it. There are two sides to every story, and all we have right now is one side. We need to get your version so we can get the truth working for you rather than against you.

The investigator has made the accusation and now has the goal of obtaining an admission. Investigators can achieve this only if they provide the suspect with an acceptable reason to confess. This sales pitch, argument, or theme must in some fashion answer the suspect's question, "What's in it for me?"

> **Nobody confesses without having a reason to do so.**

Although interrogators have many arguments from which to choose, they base most of them on one of three principles or a combination of these principles. To select the proper approach, the interrogator must decide what that particular suspect will accept at that particular time. It need not make sense to anybody else, just that suspect.

Redirect Blame

Nobody likes to take the blame for things that have gone wrong. A school principal might use this idea by saying to a student:

> Listen son, I'm not trying to put the blame on you. If you hadn't gotten mixed up with those guys, you would never have trashed that classroom. I'm sure it wasn't your idea.

> **Blame everybody except the suspect.**

Just as the principal did in the above example, if you can present an argument in a way that blames somebody or something else, the suspect might confess. Interrogators can use this technique in many situations. For instance, the investigator who confronted the rapist in the scenario mentioned previously might continue as follows:

> As I said, there is no question you're the person she is talking about. There are two sides to every story, but all we have now is her version. Although I'm not trying to excuse what you did, I don't think it was all your fault.
>
> I don't think that you just randomly grabbed her and raped her. My guess is you met her as she was leaving the bar, and you struck up a conversation with her. She probably seemed more than a little friendly. Couple that with the way she was dressed, and I can see how anybody could get the wrong idea. I saw how she looked, and it looked like she was on the make to me.
>
> Things get going pretty good, and all of a sudden she changes the rules and tells you to stop. Hell, we all know that "stop" often means "go," and I'm guessing that's what you thought.
>
> Only afterwards did you realize that maybe she really meant for you to stop. Now that doesn't make what you did right, but she's certainly got to take her share of the blame. However, that's not going to happen as long as you continue to be stupid enough to insist you were home alone watching television. We need to get the truth working for you, so let's get both sides of the story on the record.

Although the above argument does not provide a legal defense, it does offer the suspect a face-saving explanation; the victim caused it. Furthermore, it reinforces the accusation put forth by the interrogator by showing that the suspect's current strategy will not work. Often, this approach will produce an admission.

The interrogator has decided that blaming somebody or something else, in this case the victim, offers the best chance of obtaining a confession. The interrogator must expound upon and repeat this idea again and again. Persistence produces results. A confession does not result from an idea presented in one paragraph; it results from an idea that the interrogator enlarges into a story. The interrogator must paint an acceptable picture using words. In this case, the words portray the victim as a tease and the suspect as a victim.

Provide a Good Motive or Intention

People often fall back on the disclaimer, "You don't understand," when all other efforts to avoid responsibility for their actions fail. They usually follow this statement with an explanation justifying their behavior. Truth seekers, be they truant officers or detectives, can take advantage of this tendency by encouraging this rationalization:

> Billy, when you left home this morning, I'm sure you had every inten-
> tion of coming to school. You got sidetracked for a couple of minutes
> and the next thing you know, it's too late. By coming that late you
> would have caused more problems than you would by not showing up
> at all. I believe you really stayed out because you didn't want to cause
> a big scene in the middle of the school day.

Although this attempt to interpret a person's actions in a self-serving fashion does not excuse the misdeed, it can make it much more palatable. Good
interrogators can suggest an acceptable motive or intention for an otherwise
unacceptable action that lets the suspect know that they do understand. This
often provides all the motivation needed to obtain an admission. For example,
the interrogator might say to the rape suspect:

> . . . no doubt that you are involved. However, there's also no doubt in
> my mind that that's not what you intended. You show up at the bar just
> as she is leaving and engage her in conversation, The next thing you
> know, you seem to be getting along just fine. She's not much of a look-
> er, but what the hell. So you decide to do her a favor. Soon the body
> is on automatic pilot, and instinct takes over. At this point it doesn't
> matter what she says or does.

> Yeah, you forced her, but that's not the point. The point is you didn't
> calculate this. You started out trying to be nice to her because she
> really looked like she could use a friend. Then you got caught up in
> the heat of passion and lost your head. There's no doubt in my mind
> that's how it happened.

Poor:	**You should not have stolen the money.**
Better:	**I'm sure you intended to put it back.**

The interrogator offers no legal defense with this sales pitch but does provide
a conscience-soothing device. It allows the suspect to look in the mirror without
seeing a villain. Often the interrogators must supply this justification and then sell
its acceptability. They cannot count on their suspect to do it for them.

Reduce the Magnitude

The tactic of minimizing the nature of the offense can be heard in every
venue from kindergarten to retirement homes. The culprits do not try to deny
their acts. Instead, they strive to diminish the seriousness of their deeds to an
acceptable level of culpability. The employee suspected of theft might say:

It's not like my taking these office supplies is going to bankrupt the company. It would be different if I were taking a bunch of stuff and then selling it. I'm only taking enough for my own use, and besides, the company gets it wholesale.

> **Compared to murder, all other crimes are minor.**

Again, this provides no legal defense, just a face-saving excuse. Interrogators can sometimes use this technique by tailoring an argument to fit a particular crime:

> . . . no doubt that you did this. However, let's take a minute and put this in perspective. I've been in this business a long time and let me tell you, this ain't a big deal. Nobody even got hurt. Most of the cases I work on start with a dead, mutilated body. That's the kind of thing that everybody thinks of when they hear the term, "sex offender."
>
> Unfortunately, the allegation against you technically fits the same category. It's not fair, but that's the way it is. Even though you didn't kill anybody, didn't mutilate anybody, didn't hurt anybody at all, you are going to be lumped into the same group as some hard-core perverts.
>
> Many people have a tendency to think the worst of others. I don't know why, but maybe it makes them feel better about themselves. Don't let yourself be treated that way; give your side of the story. Yeah, you had sex with her, and maybe she did ask you to stop. If so, you should have. I'm not trying to excuse what you did.
>
> However, sex is a perfectly natural act, and there's nothing evil about it. You're not a pervert, but unless you give your version of what happened, that's what everybody is going to think.

Minimizing murder would require a great deal of creativity. "You only killed four people; it could have been a hundred." Even P.T. Barnum would have had trouble selling that line. However, interrogators can minimize any other crime by comparing it to murder:

> Nobody died here; if they had, it would be all over for you. Anything else, we can always straighten out. Thank heaven you had sense enough not to kill anyone.

Phase Three: Prevent Denials

Usually even the guilty ultimately will offer some sort of denial during the argument phase of the interrogation. One such denial is acceptable if made

> **The more a suspect says "No," the more difficult it becomes for him or her to say "Yes."**

immediately after the accusation because it gives the interrogator a chance to evaluate its validity. However, after this denial, allow no more. Cut them off. Furthermore, after beginning the argument, tolerate no denials at all. Otherwise these denials will reinforce the suspect's will to resist, making confession all the more difficult. It puts the suspect in the position of having to make two admissions, being a criminal and being a liar. The interrogator might prevent this by using the following technique:

Suspect:	I'm telling you I didn't . . .
Interrogator:	We've gone beyond that now. It's not a question of did you do it. It's where do we go from here that matters. What we need to do is . . .
Suspect:	Could I say something here?
Interrogator:	When I'm finished, yes. Right now I want you to listen to me. What we need to do is . . .

If for some reason the interrogator has misread the suspect and has accused an innocent person, the interrogation will never progress beyond this point. Innocent people will not tolerate a narrative whose message consists of an explanation about why they should confess. Each attempt to proceed will meet with a firmer denial until, finally, the suspect refuses to listen any further. The guilty, however, are not so easily insulted. In a mistaken effort to appear innocent, they feign excessive tolerance of all accusations. They will attempt to debate with the interrogator and will try to interject a denial any time the interrogator pauses. If this fails, they often will seek permission to interrupt with questions such as: "Can I say something here?" If granted this request, they will immediately offer another denial.

Phase Four: Defeat Protests

When their denials fail, the guilty may resort to issuing protests. They may resemble the following:

Mom, you know I wouldn't take the cookies. I don't know why you are accusing me of it because I can't even reach the cookie jar.

Note that the child has not denied taking the cookies. Instead, he has given an explanation of why he seemingly could not have taken the cookies. Usually this protest contains enough truth to enable the accused to self-righteously defend it if someone disputes it. The guilty welcome this because it allows them to argue a technicality rather than defend their innocence. Interrogators who have managed to prevent denials must remain alert for this shift in strategy, or they will find themselves involved in a losing argument. In the previous example, the child really could not reach the cookie jar. However, by using a chair, he could—and did.

Suspect:	**I wouldn't hurt him, I love my kids.**
Poor:	**He didn't get those bruises by himself.**
Better:	**That's why we must not let this happen again.**

Perpetrators of more serious transgressions will often use the same ploy once they have found that denials do not work. Instead of disputing the protests, interrogators should agree with them. This disarms and frustrates the suspects because they do not get the debate they hoped for and anticipated. The interrogators can then use this agreement to further develop the argument being presented:

Suspect: I wouldn't rape that woman or anybody else; I wasn't raised like that. I grew up in a religious environment.

Interrogator: I know you did. I've checked your background. That's why I'm taking the time to get your side of the story. You're not some scumbag whose life consists of preying on people. What you are is basically a decent guy who got carried away.

You know, there are many aspects to religion, the part you referred to that sets out rules of behavior, and the other that has to do with forgiveness. There is nothing that can't be forgiven if we are sorry for what we have done.

However, nobody can repent anything without first admitting his mistake. That's where you are right now. I'm here not to punish you but to help you see the light and get this behind you as I know your religious background taught you to do.

This type of response to a suspect's protest often produces a reaction of bewilderment, a sort of: "What went wrong here? What do I do now? I've tried denying, and I've tried debating, and I've gotten nowhere. What do I do now?" Answers to these questions do not come easily to the suspect.

Phase Five: Foiling Escapism

"Don't ignore me! Look at me when I'm talking to you!" Parents, school-teachers, and other adults serving as disciplinarians have used this command through the years. They know that nothing they say will change the errant child's behavior if it does not register. Good interrogators know the same thing.

> **"Yes, dear" from a spouse does not mean that you have been heard.**

When neither their denials nor protests succeed, most suspects would like to bolt from the situation. However, they cannot because this would remove the facade of innocence they hope to maintain. They can, however, attempt to mentally escape from the interrogation. This withdrawal takes the form of a trance-like expression, indicative of an invisible barrier that they have constructed. Comedian Carol Burnett, while lecturing her young daughter about some wrongdoing, was pleasantly surprised at how attentive the child remained even though Ms. Burnett had droned on interminably. Finally, convinced that she had suitably reformed the child, she paused and asked if her daughter had any questions. Her daughter replied, "Mommy, how many teeth do you have?"

As interrogators resume their arguments after cutting off denials and thwarting protests, they must remain alert for this mental escape attempt and deal with it. To get through to suspects in this state, interrogators may have to address them by their first names and reduce the distance between themselves and the subjects, perhaps actually touching them in a supportive, comforting way. Keeping the sales pitch simple and pressing it home through repetition will also help keep the suspect listening and involved.

Phase Six: Offer a Good/Bad Option

Most people enjoy having choices because it gives them the feeling of being in control. They do not like the idea of being compelled to do something. On the other hand, having too many choices can produce indecision. Merchants, such as car dealers, often use this paradox to sell their products:

You know you have to buy a new car because yours is on its last legs, and it's just not worth putting more money into it. You don't want to be throwing good money after bad. The question is, do you take the plunge now, while they are on sale, so you can save a bunch of money, or do you try to hold off and end up back in here next week after the factory rebate offer has expired?

I can still give you my same discount then, but the rebate is beyond my control; this is the last week. Do you want to come in next week and spend an additional $1,000.00 or do you want to save it by making the deal now? You don't want to waste the money, do you? You do want to get the $1,000.00 rebate don't you?

To close the deal, the car salesperson did not ask whether the customer wanted to buy a car. Instead, he gave the customer two choices, each of which involved the purchase of a car. The option resulted from the amount of additional savings one choice offered when compared to the other. If presented at the right moment, when the buyer's resistance has weakened, a sale will often take place. Proper timing precludes the potential customer from recognizing a third choice, not to buy a car at all, or at least not to buy one from the dealer making the pitch.

Interrogators, just like car salespeople, can take advantage of this human tendency to select from two options if one seems significantly better than the other:

As I said, you didn't go there and lay in wait for the woman after stalking her for weeks and weeks. If you had I wouldn't be wasting my time with you. That kind of behavior would put you in the category of an animal who should be locked up forever.

But that's not what happened, is it? You had a chance encounter and after getting led on by her, you just reacted on the spur of the moment. If you had had time to think about it in the light of day, it would never have happened. You didn't plan this, did you? It was just a spur-of-the-moment thing, wasn't it?

This approach offers the suspect only two alternatives. One portrays the suspect as a despicable, conniving low-life not worthy of anything but the harshest treatment, while the other paints him as an unfortunate victim of circumstances. The latter offers a conscience-soothing image and also a ray of hope for leniency from the system.

Poor:	**You can tell me.**
Better:	**Did you intend to hurt him that badly?**
Best:	**You just tried to teach him a lesson, right?**

When viewed clinically, it may seem unrealistic to expect a suspect to accept the lesser of the two evils presented. To presume that the suspect would not recognize that other choices exist seems unreasonable.

Fortunately, the interrogation room is not a laboratory devoid of emotion. Rather, it teems with anger, hope, fear, desperation, and other emotions too numerous to list. By using these emotions, interrogators can sometimes create an atmosphere in which the suspect will grasp at any positive suggestion, however slight. Interrogators can do this by:

- convincingly accusing the suspect

- preventing denials

- redirecting protests

- foiling the suspect's mental escape

- watching for the onset of receptive signs

- offering a good/bad option

Warren Holmes, a polygrapher and lecturer, during a presentation regarding interrogation, received a challenge by a member of the audience. The challenger said that this sales pitch approach to interrogation might work when applied to somebody with a conscience or when used against the inexperienced criminal, but that against a hardened street criminal, it would invariably fail. The student suggested that someone of this type, arrested on suspicion of robbery, would never confess unless confronted with overwhelming proof of guilt.

Mr. Holmes acknowledged that nothing will work every time, but this should not prevent a person from trying because not trying guarantees failure. He proposed that in the case presented to him, the interrogator might offer the following:

> Jimmy, I've advised you of your rights, but I'm not going to ask you any questions right now. What I want you to do is just sit there and listen to me for a few minutes. I want to tell you a few things about armed robbery.
>
> You know, in all my years in law enforcement, I never met anybody who as a kid said, "When I grow up I want to be a robber." No kid starts out like that. He starts out hanging around on the corner with his buddies with not a damn thing to do. There aren't a whole lot of little leagues and tennis clubs for kids in his neighborhood. If he is going to have any fun, he has to create it on his own.
>
> As early as age six or seven, he figures out that stealing from the corner store is kind of fun, and it doesn't even matter if he takes something he wants; it's a kick to steal it whether he needs it or not. The thrill of this doesn't last long, however, and before long he's looking for something with a little more excitement to it than shoplifting. So

maybe he tries burglarizing a few cars, takes a few hubcaps, lifts a radio, anything that he can get. Again, not because he wants it, but because it's a kick to do it. The thrill of this soon wears off, too.

He may graduate to going to the park at night, roughing up a few teenagers, maybe getting a few bucks from them. He might next progress to house burglary; now there *is* a kick. To go into some-body's house at night, knowing the owner is in there, can really get the adrenaline going. But even this finally loses its charm.

Finally he gets to the point that in order to get the same rush he once got from shoplifting a candy bar, he now must walk into a store, point a gun in a guy's face and have him do whatever he tells him to. You know why that's such a kick? Because it represents control and power, and that's a rush for almost everybody. Generals, corporate presidents, and stickup artists all have one thing in common—they get a kick out of being in charge. They don't just want it, they need it.

But I haven't told you a thing you don't already know. You are there right now. You didn't start out with the intention of being what you are; it just happened. You know that, too. However, let me tell you a couple of things about armed robbery that you don't know.

You know what the average take for a stickup is these days, including bank robberies? It's less than $217 per robbery. That isn't much when you consider the risk involved. You want to know how long the aver-age career lasts for an armed robber? Seventeen months—that's less than a year and a half. You know where the robber is after 17 months? In jail for life or dead. Let me tell you why.

Sometime within that 17 months, the robber is going to go into a store and tell the guy behind the counter to freeze, and the guy won't do it. Instead, he reaches for a gun. Hell, everybody out there has one, and statistics show that in less than a year and a half, one of them will reach for it rather than do what he is told. When this happens, it is over for the robber. Either he gets blown away and gets buried, or he shoots the shop owner. Those are the only choices, and both of them are losing propositions. We don't solve all our stickups, but we solve our murders, and we put the killers in jail for life.

That's where you are right now, on the brink of going to jail for life or going to a grave, and there isn't a thing you can do about this by yourself. You are in a vicious circle that escalates to only one outcome. You didn't want it; you didn't ask for it; and it mostly wasn't your fault, but you're stuck with it. You can't escape from it without help. It takes professional help to break this circle when it's gone this far.

Unfortunately for you, there is a price. There can be no help without admitting to the problem, and that's going to get your wrist smacked for you. Sure you're going to go to jail for awhile, but that's where the help is. I'm not talking about having you make license plates for a few years, I'm talking about real help.

It's really up to you. You can acknowledge you have a problem and get some help, or you take one of the other alternatives, life in prison or death. You really would prefer to get this problem straightened out and get on with your life, wouldn't you? You don't want to be dead or in jail forever, do you? You do have a problem you want help with, don't you?

This argument has a chance of succeeding because it contains at least some elements of truth that the suspect can recognize. It also provides something of an answer to the all-important question, "What's in it for me?"

Summary

Having concluded that a suspect is guilty, an interrogator must then provide that suspect with acceptable reasons to confess. Just as interviews follow a pattern, so do interrogations. They begin with an accusation, which is followed by a sales pitch. Although interrogators must tailor these appeals to specific suspects and crimes, most pitches do at least one of the following: Place the blame on something besides the suspect, downplay the seriousness of the crime, or provide an acceptable motive for the crime. During this process, the interrogator must thwart denials and protests, ensure that the suspect is listening, look for indicators that the suspect is accepting the pitch, and then present the suspect with an option question to which every answer constitutes an admission.

Suggested Reading

Inbau, Fred E. and John E. Reid (1986). *Criminal Interrogations and Confessions*. Baltimore, MD: Williams and Wilkins.

Rabon, Don (1992). *Interviewing and Interrogation*. Durham, NC: Carolina Academic Press.

Chapter 8
Keys to Success

The information previously presented regarding accusation, sales pitch, denials, excuses, escapism, and a good/bad option seems rather simplistic and straightforward. Despite this, however, far too few members of the law enforcement community achieve much success in obtaining confessions. Those who do obviously have acquired skills and insights that many investigators lack. Isolating and examining what these few do differently may reveal what makes a good interrogator.

Influence

During a lecture, Ted Smith, a communications professor at Virginia Commonwealth University suggested that people can only motivate others by one of three means: power, attractiveness, or persuasion. Although civilizations since the beginning of recorded time have wrestled with this problem, none has mastered it.

The problem stems from the need for the speaker to convince an audience, whether it is a group of voters listening to a politician or a suspect listening to an interrogator, that the speaker has credibility, an attribute consisting of two elements: trust and competence. Without trust, the audience has no reason to accept what the speaker says as truth. Without competence, the audience has no basis to accept it as accurate. Philosophers may debate which element is more critical. However, good interrogators know that they must have both.

> **We do not buy things from people we do not trust.**

Everything presented up to this point regarding interrogation presupposes that the interrogator has accrued at least some degree of credibility. Without it, no sales pitch or any other technique, no matter how innovative, will produce the desired confession. Unfortunately, others must bestow this credibility; it is in the eye of the beholder. We cannot decree that we have it. Saying "Trust me, I'm with the government, and I'm here to help you," will not automatically produce credibility. Such statements are often counterproductive and fit the same category as "Have I got a deal for you!"

Audiences often award credibility based on how you look and how you sound. Height, build, age, appearance, demeanor, and how you speak, particularly in the early stages of an encounter, may matter more than what you say. Those who work extensively on their opening lines are misplacing their efforts. The words do not count for much; the delivery style and the delivery system mean much more.

> **Packaging sells products, so look and sound professional.**

Characteristics that credible people often possess include: a perceived organization, a calm and confident demeanor, and perhaps most important, a controlled, well-modulated voice. The absence of these traits can result in the audience seeing the speaker in the same light as Barney Fife or a con artist.

Power

Power offers the most effective and efficient method of influencing others. The perceived ability to reward and punish can get things done. Suppose that an individual tells another to stand up and then shoots that person for failing to respond quickly enough. The next person ordered to stand up will do so very quickly because having a gun and displaying a willingness to use it is power in its most primitive form. Power may cause resentment, usually will produce compliance, and may require continued surveillance, but it does work.

> **Threats don't get confessions.**

In the past, the effectiveness of power caused some police officers to overuse it as a motivator. After all, it had worked on the beat. When he told the street punks to move along or suffer the consequences, they moved or wished they had. The next time they were told to move, they moved. Many officers patrolling a beat learned this lesson early and had it reinforced often.

Unfortunately, when viewed in the context of an interrogation, power plays a very small part. Constitutional restrictions preclude the use of physical power.

"Don't move or I'll shoot," can be a legitimate command during an arrest. However, "Confess or I'll beat your brains out with this phone book," is outside the legal scope of the interrogator's options.

Attractiveness

If people find you attractive enough, or like you enough, they will do almost anything for you, often without you even asking. They may even attempt to anticipate your desires and meet them ahead of time. They will often do things they would prefer not to do just because they like you. They may find you attractive on a heroic scale as a sports star or film star; on a status scale as a doctor or a police officer; or on a personal level as a friend. No matter which scale, this attractiveness, although limited in application, can be very powerful.

To show just how powerful, suppose you want to make a lot of money selling a good but overpriced product. Add to this the premise that your potential customers can buy similar but less expensive products elsewhere. How can you make your fortune under these circumstances? Mr. Tupper figured it out. He had to, because competitors offered similar but cheaper products. Therefore, Mr. Tupper did not attempt to have his employees sell his products. Instead, he provided customers with an opportunity to host a party. Not only would the people have a party, they would receive "free" gifts for doing so.

The strategy continues to work year after year. People giving the party invite their friends who attend whether they want to or not because they do not want to turn down a friend. During the party, the host, not the company representative, mingles among the party-goers with a stack of order forms, and everybody feels compelled to buy something, including people who may already own some of these products.

Despite the influence that people can wield over those who like them, this factor has limited application in the interview and interrogation process. We have little control over whether others will like us, and what influence we do have takes longer to achieve than the average investigator can devote to any one individual. Long-term influencing efforts—such as informant development—offer a better chance for success using attractiveness as a motivator.

Persuasion

Many interrogation instructors receive inquiries regarding the latest developments and most innovative techniques in their field. They often respond by suggesting that nothing has yet replaced persuasion as the most effective method for obtaining confessions. By *persuasion* they mean establishing credibility and then providing logical or emotional reasons for the person to behave in a certain way. Although it sounds simple, applying it involves an infinite number of variables that interrogators must consider. They must have an understanding of human nature and use it to: (1) select the optimum time and location, (2) set the scene appropriately, (3) choose the proper approach, and (4) maintain enough flexibility to adapt and change when it becomes apparent that their original ideas are not working. The ability to consistently meet these challenges defines the true professional who understands all of the following topics and many others.

The Setting

Previous discussion of the best location for an interview suggested that the number of variables precludes making any definitive recommendations. Homes, offices, neutral sites—all offer advantages under certain circumstances. However, for an interrogation, fewer variables apply. Although interrogators may suggest subtle differences regarding the ideal environment for an interrogation, most of them generally agree on the type of setting they desire.

The Room

Successful interrogators suggest using a small room that has few distractions. It should have few, if any, law enforcement trappings and certainly nothing that hints at punishment.

Furniture

Some disagree about whether an interrogation room should contain a desk. However, few, if any, suggest that interrogators position themselves behind the desk and place the suspect in front of it. Although occasionally this can produce the desired effect, usually this superior/subordinate arrangement makes the interrogation process more difficult. Many prefer limiting the furniture to two straight-backed chairs placed facing one another, about four feet apart.

Those who prefer a desk suggest that the interrogator position the chairs so that they face one another with only a corner of the desk partially interposed between them. This enables the interrogator to observe the suspect's body movements while still providing a modest level of security that a barrier offers. The desk can also provide a stable writing surface, if needed.

Props

Interrogators unanimously view distractions as counterproductive, but props, particularly if visual, can contribute significantly to a successful interrogation. Two of the main types are those designed to enhance the prestige of the interrogator, such as framed awards and commendations, and those designed to convince the suspect of the futility of continued resistance. The latter can include piles of real or implied evidence, such as items taken from the crime scene, enlarged surveillance photographs, and file folders and drawers with the name of the suspect clearly visible. Evidence tags scattered liberally on these items can also have an effect. Often interrogators will place these items in an inconspicuous location so the suspect will "discover" them. These discoveries will have greater impact than if the interrogator blatantly displays them or calls them to the suspect's attention.

> **Props, like pictures, can be worth a thousand words.**

Years ago, an FBI agent placed a suspect's name on three drawers of a five-drawer file cabinet. He labeled the other two drawers "Watergate" and "Abscam," two very high-profile cases at the time. Apparently, the government had devoted three times the space to him as it had to either of these nationally known matters. This produced a very sobering effect, and the suspect immediately began asking about what considerations he might receive in return for cooperation.

Most interrogators want no visible telephone in the interrogation room because it can remind the suspect that he might summon help. Also, a phone ringing at an inopportune moment can destroy hours of effort. However, some prefer having a telephone, minus the ringer, available at least during the interview phase. If the suspect agrees or even suggests a willingness to take a polygraph exam, his reaction to the interrogator's immediate attempt to reach the examiner will often reveal the suspect's degree of sincerity. Many guilty suspects will offer to take a polygraph as a stalling tactic. They assume it will occur at a future date, and that they can deal with it then. A guilty suspect who does this will often show a significant change in demeanor when the interrogator offers an immediate test. At this point, the interrogator's confidence in the suspect's guilt should soar.

Only case circumstances and the imagination of the investigator will limit the use of props. Effective use of them can sometimes make the difference between success and failure in the interrogation room.

Argument Selection

Whether trying to convince a customer to buy a product or a suspect to tell the truth, the chance of success increases with the appropriateness of the sales pitch. Many lost sales result from trying to use the same pitch with every customer, and interrogators lose many confessions using the same approach with every suspect. The following is a sample of a vastly overused, generic sales pitch:

> You know, what you are doing here is really stupid. If you think sitting here telling me you didn't do it is going to make it so, you're just being foolish. We've already got enough evidence to arrest you, and it's only a matter of time until we'll have enough evidence to put you away for years.
>
> Right now you have a chance to help yourself. Once we have all the pieces put together, and that won't be long, it will be too late for you. As the guy who sells oil filters says, "You can pay me now, or you can pay me later." The difference will be in how much it costs. I suggest you tell us now while you can still do yourself some good. Pay us now before the cost goes up.

This "oil filter" sales pitch, "You can pay me now or pay me later," although it has nearly universal application no matter what the crime, often does not produce an admission of guilt. Unfortunately, many interrogations begin and end with this theme. If it does not succeed, the interrogators fail because they know no other approach. Good interrogators usually will begin with an argument more tailored to the specific suspect and crime. Doing so increases the chance of success.

The ability to select the proper argument often distinguishes successful interrogators from the unsuccessful interrogators. Usually, they attribute this ability to intuition, the old "gut reaction." What they regard as intuition is often the subconscious processing of information received from various sources such as records, case files, and interviews.

Poor:	Quit worrying about it.
Better:	It will be okay.
Best:	We'll take care of it.

Most suspects who refuse to confess do so because they fear that something bad will happen. Recognizing the specific fear often enables an interrogator to present a theme aimed at reducing this inhibition. The variety of fears is limitless. Suspects may fear such things as: losing their jobs, going to jail, embarrassing themselves or their families, losing what they stole, looking like a snitch, or receiving the death penalty. The interrogator should identify the suspect's fears; successful interrogators do.

Many investigators experience frustration when they try to reduce what their common sense tells them should be the suspect's main fear. Unfortunately, logic often has little to do with the suspect's thought process. Interrogators often fail to listen to the suspect and thus fail to discover his or her real concerns. Although they may hear the suspect's words, they cannot or will not accept them. This often results in an exchange similar to the following:

Interrogator: I need to get your side of the story. I think you acted on the spur of the moment. If you planned this, you could be facing a death sentence. I don't think you deserve that, but I need your help to establish that.

Suspect: I don't want to go to jail tonight for something I didn't do.

Interrogator: I don't want to put you in the gas chamber for something you didn't plan.

Suspect: If I say I did it, are you going to put me in jail tonight?

Interrogator: I can't say; that's beyond my control, but I do know that manslaughter or even second degree murder beats the hell out of walking that last mile.

Suspect: I know I waived my right to an attorney, and I meant it. However, if I say I want an attorney, can I stay here till he comes rather than being put in a cell?

Interrogator: No, you cannot, and I can't promise what an attorney will do. However, I do know there is nobody on death row who got there without an attorney.

The investigator in this case has allowed logic, reason, and a normal sense of priorities to get in the way of hearing what the suspect regards as important. With many criminals, only the short term or the immediate future matters. Fear of going to jail that night looms foremost in this suspect's mind. To most people, a night in jail pales in comparison to the death penalty, but this does not matter because only the suspect counts in this situation. Good investigators know this and try to allay the suspects' fears rather than addressing the fears that logic would suggest:

Interrogator: I'm not interested in causing you any extra problems; in fact, I'm willing to work with you as long as it takes to get this resolved. It's getting late, but I'm willing to spend all night here if that's what it takes. There is no way we can finish this up before morning gets here. I can certainly say that finding out the whole truth regarding this matter will keep you from being put in a cell tonight. It is very important that we get the whole truth, don't you think?

Suspect: You're right, and I didn't plan it, and I didn't mean to kill him. He made me so damn mad that without thinking, I grabbed the poker from the fireplace and hit him with it.

The suspect has now begun to focus on the initial appeal and to see the logic of accepting it. However, this occurred only after the interrogator put the fear of immediate lockup to rest. Interrogators must not allow their own value systems to cloud their understanding of a suspect. If they do, they will usually fail.

A bank teller suspected of significant embezzlements confessed to an interrogator who offered to take care of her cat. An arsonist confessed when assured that his crime would not be a front-page story. A burglar confessed when assured he would not have to wear prison clothes before being sentenced. A juvenile admitted to murder when told that the investigator would explain things to his parents. None of these would have occurred if the interrogators had insisted on using the generic sales pitch, "Pay me now or pay me later."

Most people are familiar with the golden rule, "Do unto others as you would have others do unto you," and in theory it has merit. However, when it comes to motivating others, the golden rule succeeds only when the "doer" and the "doee" want the same treatment. Usually the value systems of law enforcement officers vary significantly from that of the average suspect. Appealing to values that are important to themselves rather than to the suspect prevents many interrogators from obtaining confessions.

> **A bartender cannot stock only his or her favorite brand of alcohol.**

To illustrate why this happens, you need only look at how the perceptions of law enforcement personnel differ from those of criminals. Many instruments developed to measure personality traits, value systems, communication styles, and other facets of human nature illustrate these differences. Although each instrument has its own nuances, most have many aspects in common.

One such instrument, developed by psychologists David Keirsey and Marilyn Bates, categorizes people into four temperaments, two of which equally divide 76 percent of the population. Amazingly, however, based on results provided by many groups of police officers and FBI agents, more than 80 percent of them fall into one category. Keirsey and Bates have termed those of this temperament *Guardians,* people who value stability and tradition. A sense of duty and a need to serve motivate this group. These characteristics seem to cause many of them to select and remain in law enforcement. These *Guardians* also rely on this set of values when attempting to influence the behavior of others:

> Joe, there's no doubt that you were involved in ripping off the insurance company, and you're going to have to face the consequences for your actions. However, you didn't do it by yourself, and we need to know who the others were.

I've checked your background and I know you were raised in an environment that taught you right from wrong. I also know that you spent a couple of years in the military and got an honorable discharge. Based on this, it should be easy for you to see why we need to get the truth. Unless rules are followed, our society would break down and things would be in chaos. Each of us has a duty to see that this does not happen.

Right now you're thinking in terms of not being a rat regarding your friends. Let me tell you a few things: first, they are not your friends to get you in a fix like this. You don't owe them a thing. Second, you have a duty to do your part to keep this society together. You need to face this like a man and do the right thing as you were raised and trained to do.

To most law enforcement personnel, this argument makes complete sense. Everybody has a duty to do whatever possible to make the world a better place. They learned this at home and had it reinforced by various social institutions such as the church, school, scouts, and the military. Thus, an interrogator might think: "How can anybody not see this? Everybody knows this. I'm merely verbalizing the obvious so the suspect will find it easy to agree."

Unfortunately, the above assumptions do not have universal application. Although everyone may understand the words being spoken, to much of the population, this appeal to duty falls on unreceptive ears. It often produces a response such as:

I don't have any idea what you're talking about. Besides, I don't owe anybody a thing. What has society ever done for me?

When this happens and no confession results, the typical officer reverts to the "pay me now or pay me later" theme. If this fails, the interrogator often quits.

The urge to persuade or motivate others by using our own value systems has great appeal. We have difficulty grasping the idea that something so important to us would have so little effect on somebody else. Instead, if unsuccessful, we often assume that they must not have heard or understood us. We therefore repeat ourselves, usually at a higher volume. Not recognizing that other value systems dominate the world in general and the criminal world in particular has caused many interrogators to fail.

> **Regardless of your values, they represent a minority.**

Just as Guardians make up 38 percent of the general population but dominate law enforcement, another group, identified by Keirsey and Bates as *Artisans,* also make up 38 percent of the general population and seem to dominate the criminal element. They do so because their temperament inclines them to do things just for the joy of doing them. Although any profession may attract someone of this temperament, most Artisans gravitate to professions that provide opportunity for freedom and spontaneity. What profession can offer more freedom than one that requires no adherence to any rules? Most criminals choose their way of life because of the freedom and thrills that such a life provides. The interrogator must use something besides duty and honor to appeal to these people:

> Sure you were involved in ripping off the insurance company; that's not the question. You're going to be convicted and sentenced, and you're going to do your time. The question is, how are you going to do that time? I'm not offering you any deal such as a shorter sentence or better conditions, but I will give you a chance to do more than just sit on your behind for your entire jail term.
>
> As you probably know, the prison where you would go if you plead has lots of problems, both with the inmates and the staff. I could use a source inside to give me some information, and you would be good at it if you wanted to be. It wouldn't be easy however. You would have to sell yourself to a bunch of dangerous men who wouldn't hesitate to kill you. It sure would be a kick, though.
>
> I could provide you with a code name, and we can work out how we can pull this off. We'll have to develop a system so we can communicate. However, I can't do a thing until your current charges are resolved. Why don't you just tell me the whole story, and we can go from there?

Upon hearing the script above, many law enforcement officers would scoff in disbelief. This pitch falls so far outside their value system that not only would they not accept such an appeal, they cannot fathom anyone doing so. As a result, given the temperament of most criminals, these officers will never become effective interrogators. Instead, they will continue to stress the qualities of common sense, duty, and honor. These qualities really do not make much of an impression on the typical criminal. Offering them something that appeals to their desire for excitement and adventure has a better chance of success.

Sales Strategies

In his book, *Influence,* Robert Cialdini discusses various techniques used by merchants to trigger acceptance of their products. He tries to alert his readers to these tactics so they can avoid buying things that they do not really want. Although interrogators sell the idea of confession rather than a product, they can often use many of the same ploys. These techniques use persuasion—after establishing credibility, one must provide logical or emotional reasons to motivate people to act as desired.

Social Acceptance

Humans sometimes have the tendency to attribute acceptability to anything done by enough people. After all, how could that many people be wrong? This results in advertisements such as:

> Of all of the cigarettes on the market today, Ol' Lung Busters is the number one selling brand. Don't stay on the outside looking in, join the crowd that's in the know.

The above statement will sell the product because it enables people to rationalize their behavior—never mind the irrefutable evidence that shows that smoking cigarettes will kill you. Interrogators also can appeal to this tendency to join the crowd by suggesting:

> Don't sit there thinking you're the only one who's done this sort of thing. I've been in this business a long time, and let me tell you, I see this sort of thing every day. I'm not saying you're right, but most people in your position would have done the same thing.

Just as with the cigarettes, it must be all right if everyone is doing it. This approach can sell cigarettes, confessions, and many other improbable things. People "go along to get along," from something as silly as having their ears pierced to something as tragic as the Jonestown mass suicide, where over 900 people got in line so they and their children could drink a cyanide-laced drink. Good interrogators recognize the power of social acceptance and use it where they can.

> **Everyone likes to hear "You're not alone."**

Urgency

A real estate dealer trying to close a deal might use the following:

> I know you're torn between buying this house and looking at some more. I can understand that the perfect house might be out there somewhere, and I'm willing to keep going as long as you wish. On the

other hand, I know for a fact that another couple will be making an offer on this one this afternoon, an offer just a few thousand dollars below the asking price. I believe the owner will accept it. If you want this one, you'd better grab it now because it's not likely to be here tomorrow.

How many of us have made purchases based on the premise that if we did not act at once, we would lose the opportunity? By creating an artificial deadline, often with no factual basis, merchants speed up and even cause many transactions. Phrases such as, "limited offer," "while supplies last," and, "sale ends tomorrow," all serve to push potential customers into a decision. Investigators can convey this sense of urgency to a vacillating suspect who continues to weigh the pros and cons of cooperating:

> As we speak, investigation of this case is going on two fronts. Technicians from the lab are sifting through piles of evidence that may give us all the answers we need. At the same time, detectives are out beating the bushes talking to everyone who might be able to resolve this case. Once either of these groups hits paydirt, and they will, your usefulness to us is over, and the prosecutor certainly won't take your cooperation into account. I'm not making you any promises, but if you have any hope of being cut a little slack, you had better act now.

Commitment

"Rome wasn't built in a day." Many merchants know how to apply this old saying. They recognize that by getting a potential customer to first agree with them on one point, they can ultimately use this agreement to make a sale. They proceed one step at a time:

> You are interested in your daughter's future, aren't you sir? I thought you were, how could you not be? It's because of that interest that I'm here to talk to you today. In today's high-tech world, old-fashioned values often get pushed aside. These values make the difference between a totally materialistic adult and one who has her priorities in order. As you said, you are interested in her future and that's why I want to show you our collection of classic literature, literature that can help promote the values you say you want for your child.

> **"Because I said it, it must be true."**

Believe it or not, this blatant sales strategy succeeds with some regularity. It does so because the vendor manipulates the customer into proclaiming an interest in the child's future. Once proclaimed, the customer feels obligated to concur with everything said by the seller that appears to support this interest.

The seller need not have total compliance at once: "Do you want to buy some classic literature?" would not sell many books. Instead, a minor, non-threatening commitment regarding a child's value system serves as the starting point for a final agreement to purchase the product.

Interrogators can also use this principle. By obtaining a minor admission and using that as a starting point, they can ultimately arrive at the full confession. They might proceed as follows:

> Your story just doesn't make sense. For you to sit there and deny that you were at the scene where this woman says you raped her will never hold up; it's stupid. It can be verified that you were there and not at home watching TV as you claim.

> There are always two sides to every story, mitigating circumstances that make a difference regarding who is at fault. However, as long as you deny being present, none of these can be discovered. Unless shown otherwise, people have a tendency to think the worst of each other. Don't let them think the worst of you; quit being stupid; take this opportunity to give your side of the story. You were there, weren't you?

The interrogator does not try to achieve a confession at this point but merely wants the suspect to concede some point that he would not admit before. He wants the suspect to admit only that he was at the scene of the crime, something he initially denied.

Once obtained, the interrogator can use this concession to continue in a step-by-step process to obtain additional admissions. At best, it may result in a complete confession. At worst, it has placed the suspect in the vicinity of the crime. This may suffice to convict the culprit when viewed with the other facts. The interrogator's initial willingness to accept less than a total confession can often achieve the ultimate goal, the truth.

Gratitude

Most people who receive favors feel indebted to those who grant them, and feel compelled to respond in kind. This may hold true even when the recipient neither requested nor wanted the initial favor. A few years ago a religious cult assigned its members to airport duty. They would accost people with the statement, "This is my gift to you," while presenting the traveler with a wilted, often mutilated flower. The recipients in turn would often donate money to them.

Observation showed what the recipients thought of these flowers. Once out of sight of the cult member, they would throw them in the nearest trash can. An accomplice of the cult member would also observe this and would retrieve the flowers for reuse as gifts to future victims.

Even gracious acceptance of a refusal can fit the category of a favor. Not making people feel guilty about declining to do something asked of them makes them feel grateful. They are more apt to grant the next request made of them. A phone call to me from a solicitor for a worthy charity will illustrate this:

> Sir, as you know, our organization is dedicated to wiping out a serious disease, one that often attacks adult males. The secret to defeating this disease is research. That costs money—money that must come from donations.

> We have determined that the best way to secure these donations is to have members of the community like yourself solicit funds from the neighborhood where they reside. If you would agree to do this for us, you would be doing a real service for us, for the community and ultimately, for yourself.

The solicitor, in building a seemingly valid case for his cause, used several ploys, each designed to make it difficult to decline his request. First, he explained the worthiness of his cause. Second, he personalized the project by portraying me as a prime benefactor. Third, he appealed to my ego by describing me as an esteemed member of the community. However, I dislike soliciting, so I offered an excuse and declined, fully expecting the solicitor to try to make me feel guilty for my refusal and then to apply pressure to get me to change my mind. Nothing could have been further from the truth:

> Don't give it a second thought, sir. I understand completely. Some of us have commitments that preclude us getting involved in such time-consuming activities. Others have personalities that make soliciting an ordeal, and I certainly wouldn't want to impose that burden on anybody.

> I'm very appreciative that you took the time to listen to what I had to say. Perhaps you might give some thought to doing it sometime in the future. By the way, while I have you on the phone, I'm also soliciting pledges from those people who are interested in helping. How much of a pledge can I put you down for this year?

The solicitor had me. Because he so graciously let me off the hook without evoking guilt, I felt extremely obligated to him. I eagerly leapt at the opportunity to repay him. I offered a pledge significantly higher than any I normally would have made.

In fact, I owed him nothing. He was a professional solicitor getting paid to raise money. He had bothered me at home to ask me to do his work for him, work that I would truly dislike. Yet I felt guilty about declining and wanted to make it up to him.

The interrogator can also use this concept of gratitude. A state trooper who worked juvenile matters attributed most of his confessions to the soft drink industry. After an initial unsuccessful attempt at obtaining a confession, he would pause and buy the suspect a soft drink. He insisted that more often than not, this seemingly insignificant gift resulted in a complete change in attitude and demeanor that ultimately led to a confession.

> **Put suspects in your debt, and they will often pay up.**

Interrogators can use less blatant, but similar approaches with more sophisticated suspects. This can include the strategy of graciously relenting from the demand for a confession to an exaggerated crime:

> Over the past few months approximately $40,000 worth of merchandise has been taken from this warehouse, and you're telling me you didn't do it. You know what? I believe you. There is no way you would have done that. You're not like that.
>
> There are those who want to blame you for it, though, and they have sent me in here to try to get you to admit that you did. Well, I asked you, and you said you didn't do it. I'm not going to ask you again because, as I said, I believe you.
>
> However, I am stuck with resolving this matter, and I'm pretty sure you can help. The $7,000 shipment of tools that got misdirected; that's the only part of this you had anything to do with wasn't it? Other than that, you didn't have any involvement with any missing goods, did you?

This approach does not form the entire argument as the interrogator would have presented it. The argument may have had many aspects to it, but with this one appeal, the interrogator earned the gratitude of the suspect. The interrogator did not berate, contradict, or even express a doubt about the truthfulness of the suspect's denial. Furthermore, the interrogator implied a willingness to dispute the allegation with those in authority. How can the suspect not feel grateful, and how can he repay the obligation? He could do this by admitting to the lesser and more accurate accusation.

Timing and Alternate Appeals

Interrogators must recognize the appropriate moment to present the good/bad option. It will not last indefinitely. This presentation must come when the suspect shows some vulnerability, some indicators of receptivity. Offer it too soon and it will sound like a con job. Delay too long and it will look like a last desperate attempt to obtain a confession.

If the process has gone as it should, once the interrogator has defeated the final denials and protests, no further conversation should take place. By this time, the interrogator should be presenting the sales pitch as a monologue. Therefore, the interrogator must rely on visual clues to decide when the opportune moment to deliver the good/bad option has arrived. Fortunately, nonverbal behavior provides the more reliable clues to a suspect's state of mind.

In most cases, at the time the interview becomes an interrogation, when the accusation takes place, suspects often adopt a closed, defensive posture. They fold their arms, cross their legs, and turn their bodies away from the interrogator. Interrogators obtain few, if any, confessions while suspects maintain these barriers. The interrogator must carefully watch for any relaxation of these indicators and then press home a concise sales pitch.

> **It is too difficult for the suspect to tell what he did; enable him to just nod "yes."**

As the barriers disappear, interrogators should also look for positive indicators of receptivity. A drooping of the shoulders, a nodding of the head, or the welling up of tears in the eyes can provide indications of the effectiveness of the argument. When interrogators see any of these signs, they should immediately present the good/bad option question because this receptivity may last for only a brief period. If missed, the suspects may rally their will to resist and the interrogator may have to start again.

To produce a positive response from the option question, the interrogator may have to repeat it several times. Failure to respond immediately may mean only that the suspect is thinking about the options or is preoccupied with something else. Only a heated rejection of the preferred option should signal a need to return to the sales pitch stage, either to repeat the sales pitch or to shift to a new one.

Merchants usually open their dealings with a sales pitch based on assessments of their customers. However, no matter how thoroughly they assess the potential buyers, they sometimes select the wrong approach. Consider the sales pitch that a car salesperson might use:

> I can see that you are a person who knows value. Of all the cars on the lot, and we have three acres of them, you're looking at the lowest priced car of the bunch. Why am I telling you this? You already knew that, didn't you?

> Will you take a look at that EPA figure for gas mileage? You'd have to buy a lawn mower to equal this car's engine for stinginess on fuel. Even those figures are conservative. This thing is unbelievable when it comes to economy of operation. You sure know a bargain when you see it.
>
> Let's talk repair records on this thing. We can't really, because there's nothing much to say. The reliability is outstanding. The bottom line is that from the standpoint of the initial cost, gas mileage, and repair record, you're just not going to get a better bang for the buck.

The sales pitch or theme selected by the car salesperson emphasizes economy: price, mileage, and reliability. However, if money has little meaning to this customer, stressing economy will merely waste time. If it lacks appeal, saying it again or saying it louder will not help.

The customer, free to leave, usually will do so, rarely to return. The customer who says, "I've got to check with my better half," and then departs probably will not return. The dealer has no time to waste; he must prevent the customer's departure or lose a sale. He might do this by switching to a different sales pitch, such as:

> Furthermore, this one is made right here in the U.S. It's providing jobs for Americans and boosting our economy.

The dealer has shifted to a completely new sales pitch. Patriotism has become the theme. Depending on the customer's background and the tenor of the times, this might be the approach with the best chance of success. Again the dealer must listen and watch for indicators of receptivity or rejection from the customer, either verbal or nonverbal, and react accordingly. A verbal rejection from the customer need not be blatant. It could be as mild as:

> I don't know for sure, but I'm under the impression that Mercedes, Acura, and some others are pretty much cutting edge for the automotive world.

Nonverbal indicators will probably accompany this verbal rejection. The customer probably has his arms folded, has little if any eye contact with the dealer, and may be inching toward his car for a quick getaway. The dealer must prevent this by again changing the appeal:

> Yeah, some of them are built pretty well, I guess. Before we go any further though, let me tell you that if you take this baby down to the business district at quitting time when everyone is leaving work, you just might get hurt. Women flock to this little number. This thing really does have sex appeal.
>
> Oh, really?

In addition to verbal responses, the customer may also provide some non-verbal indicators of a receptive attitude. These might include:

- shifting from a closed stance to a closer, more vulnerable one

- unfolding of the arms

- leaning forward

- nodding approval

At this point, the dealer will realize that he has found the proper sales pitch—that he has struck the right chord. He must then develop and tailor this theme to fit the self-image of the customer. When the signs of receptivity become pronounced, the dealer should present the either/or choice and press for a closing.

Interrogators must also have flexibility. If they note continued resistance to one argument, they must change to a new appeal. Consider how an interrogator might respond to a suspect who says:

> There's no way in hell I would get drunk enough to rape somebody. I've never been that drunk in my life. I had a few drinks the other night before I went out, but if you think I'm going to sit here and listen to you tell me I was so drunk I didn't know what I was doing, you'd better guess again!

The suspect has obviously rejected the interrogator's suggestion that maybe the suspect did not know what he was doing. The customer rejected the car dealer's pitch stressing economy, and the suspect rejected the interrogator's suggestion regarding diminished capacity.

Based on the suspect's specific denials, it seems certain that he had listened to the argument, he just did not accept it. The idea of projection, placing the blame on someone or something else (in this case, alcohol) for some reason lacked appeal. Although interrogators should not change themes as quickly as the car salesperson did, at some point they must make that decision:

> You know, I'm glad you said that. It gives me some additional insight into you. It tells me that you are a responsible person, not the kind who has no respect for social restraints. You are not the type of person who would deliberately get in a position where you are out of control.
>
> Because you are a responsible person, I think we need to take a look at what's happening here. You made a mistake. You exercised poor judgment, and now we have a little problem. I say little because nobody died or even got seriously hurt here. A mistake was made. Everybody makes mistakes. Nobody's perfect.
>
> Let me tell you about another guy who made a little mistake and then did not act in a responsible fashion, would not acknowledge that he had made a mistake. If he had, no big deal would have been made of

it. I'm talking about Richard Nixon, president of the United States. Now I know you're not old enough to remember, but here was a guy who had some information regarding a second-rate burglary. He had not approved of it ahead of time, but he did find out later.

Had he admitted it when the inquiries began, you know what would have happened? Nothing. He could have given his side of the story, a few wrists would have been smacked, and that would have been the end of it. But he refused to take responsibility because he could not admit he had anything to do with a stupid mistake. As a result, he ended up resigning in disgrace, not for what he did but because he could not face up to a mistake.

There's a message here. We don't want to compound the problem by refusing to take responsibility. The world was happy to believe the worst about Nixon because he could not face up to a mistake. Don't put yourself in the same boat. There are two sides to every story. Don't make the world think the worst of you. Admit your mistake and then tell your side.

The interrogator realized that placing the blame on an overindulgence of alcohol not only lacked appeal, it actually offended the suspect. The suspect became indignant at the suggestion that he would get drunk enough to lose control and act irresponsibly. Recognizing this, the interrogator not only changed sales pitches but incorporated the concept of responsibility into it. Rather than randomly moving to a new theme, the interrogator listened to the suspect and reacted accordingly. If at some point the suspect rejects this new approach, the interrogator will move to another. Just as with the car dealer and the potential customer, failure occurs only when the suspect refuses to continue with the process, or when the interrogator has nothing left to say. Therefore, the larger the repertoire of themes interrogators have, the greater their chances of success.

Summary

Because interrogators have neither the power to demand confessions nor the time to cultivate relationships that would prompt spontaneous confessions, they must persuade the guilty to admit their crimes. To do this, interrogators must first establish their credibility with the suspects and then furnish them with good reasons to confess. Selecting the proper environment, using appropriate props, and tailoring the sales pitch to the particular crime and suspect all contribute to this success.

Suggested Reading

Cialdini, Robert B. (1984). *Influence*. New York, NY: Quill Press.

Keirsey, David and Marilyn Bates (1984). *Please Understand Me*. Del Mar, CA: Prometheus Nemesis Book Company.

MacDonald, John M. and David L. Michaud (1992). *Criminal Interrogation*. Denver, CO: Apache Press.

Morris, Desmond (1994). *Body Talk*. New York, NY: Crown Publishers, Inc.

Chapter 9
Case Study

The Interrogation

Several years ago, a rarity occurred. A series of thefts took place at a law enforcement academy operated by a well-known law enforcement agency. A thief had taken money from the rooms of five or six students. None of the thefts exceeded $50. However, given the circumstances, particularly the location, academy officials considered these thefts intolerable. They wanted to solve the crime and deal with the culprit, and they began by conducting a preliminary investigation.

Academy officials operated on the premise that only custodians had ready access to the rooms and that one person probably had committed all of the thefts. They therefore reviewed the work schedules of these employees and found that only one custodian had worked on all of the dates, times, and locations of the thefts.

This person was a black female, approximately 30 years old. She was single and the mother of two small children. She was having financial difficulties and was suspected of having a drinking problem. Discreet inquiry revealed that she had no sense of loyalty to her employer, that she regarded the law enforcement agency as an elitist organization, dominated by white males with whom she had nothing in common. In her mind, all she got from it was an inadequate salary.

Theoretically, academy personnel should have conducted no further inquiry because other investigators from the agency had responsibility for such matters. However, the academy officials (former investigators) felt the urge to get back in the game one more time. They did not want to work the case; they wanted to supervise it, and they justified their actions by saying that they were merely conducting a preliminary inquiry before turning it over to the real investigators. In fact, they wanted to be able to tell the real investigators to come and pick up the case now that the academy officials had solved it.

Based on the suspect's gender, they assigned this "preliminary inquiry" to a female stationed at the academy. Law enforcement traditionally assigns females to cases that have female suspects. Never mind that research shows that absent unusual factors, of the three possibilities: male/male, female/male and female/female, the last presents the most difficult circumstance for establishing credibility.

Given limited time and resources, the investigator had few strategies from which to choose. She decided to "salt" some rooms with marked money in hopes of luring the culprit into an additional theft. This did not work, and after a couple of days, the hierarchy began to wonder how much longer this investigation would last. They invited the agent to the inner sanctum and told her they wanted this matter resolved soon. They suggested she interrogate the suspect if necessary.

The investigator, a friend of mine, asked me to take part in the interrogation. I did not want to do this because it placed me in a no-win situation. If we got a confession, people would give me no plaudits: "After all, you teach that stuff." If we failed, my credibility would be nil, "You teach interrogation and you couldn't get a confession in a simple matter like this?"

Fortunately, a colleague, Joseph Kenney, a long-time polygrapher and an outstanding interrogator, was visiting the academy while this was happening. Few people had more enthusiasm or more success doing interrogations, and he agreed to help us with this one.

He reviewed the suspect's background and then selected the office of a ranking academy official, an office with the trappings of power and prestige, as the place to conduct the interrogation. He also made some additions to the office before the suspect arrived. On a table in the corner of the room he put each wallet from which the thief had taken money. He also put eight other wallets on the table. On each wallet, he placed a yellow sticker, the type used by some courts to mark items entered as evidence. On the wall behind where he intended to sit, he hung a collage of all the departments' members who had been killed in the line of duty. This completed his preparations.

When the suspect arrived, Kenney introduced himself and then explained that some thefts, mostly of money, had taken place in some dorm rooms, that he had to get to the bottom of this matter, and he thought she might be able to help him. He then said he wanted to know a bit more about her and went on to ask her about her background, her family, and other related items. She answered the questions but volunteered very little beyond what he specifically asked. The suspect also said that she had no idea why he wanted to talk to her because she did not know anything about any missing money. She delivered this remark in a controlled but defiant manner and implied that in her mind, the interview was over.

> **If suspects don't hear you, they don't confess.**

By this time, based on what he already knew plus what he had seen and heard during this interview, Kenney had concluded that the woman had stolen the money. After some further attempts at engaging the suspect in conversation, Kenney realized the futility of such efforts. It was obvious the suspect had no intention of chatting; she consistently gave one-word answers to open-ended questions. Therefore, Kenney commenced to deliver his argument in monologue form:

> You know it's not the amount of money that's missing that is causing the problem here. It's just that they have to resolve all such items, even minor ones, and they have asked me to look into it. It's not like they're trying to put somebody in jail, it's just that they have to get to the bottom of this. They can't let these kinds of things continue. Petty as it is, it must be resolved.

> I have worked on some pretty big cases in my time, cases that resulted in a lot of people going to jail for long periods of time, but this is not one of them. All we need to do . . .

> **It's a routine crime only if someone else is being accused.**

Kenney's instincts had told him that the best theme to use was one that would reduce the importance of the offense. He reasoned that this would appeal to a person caught stealing at a law enforcement academy, particularly if in her mind, she had blown it all out of proportion. He hoped to present it as a minor indiscretion that he could put to rest without any serious repercussions.

Unfortunately, it did not work, not because of the message, but because the suspect would not listen. By watching her as he spoke, Kenney could see that she had tuned him out. She had decided that he had nothing to say that was worth hearing, nothing that had any meaning for her. Her world had nothing in common with his, and all he represented to her was somebody who was trying to get her into trouble. Kenney realized he had to remedy this and said:

> Let me tell you why this needs to be resolved. It's not the value of the things that are missing. That's a minor thing. It's because they were taken from here, and these halls are priceless. They are sacred. They're not priceless because of the cost of the concrete and steel in them but because of the price these people have paid. Do you see these guys? They paid the ultimate price; they gave their lives for what these halls stand for.

As he said this, he reached back over his shoulder and touched the photograph of the slain officers. His thumb came to rest on a particular person, one with a different characteristic than the others—he was black. As the suspect's eyes followed his gesture, her face softened and her posture became less defensive.

This strategy was not sufficient to obtain a confession; Kenney had not intended for it to do so. He used it to reduce the barrier behind which the suspect had hidden. Maybe she did have something in common with the institution after all. Kenney then returned to his theme:

As I said, even though it is a minor problem we need to get it resolved. Not only is it minor, but after talking with you plus what I already knew about you and this matter, I am convinced that you are not responsible for most of what has been going on here. There are some people who would like to blame you for everything that's been lost, borrowed, misplaced, or stolen from this academy since you got here, including money from every wallet on that table over there. I don't think so.

That's not fair and I'm going to do everything I can to see that it does not happen. You want to know why? Let me tell you. I know you have some financial problems given what they pay you here and you being single and with two young kids. It's not easy. Not only do they not pay you enough to get by on, they haven't even given any thought to offering a day care service so you wouldn't have to spend a good bit of what you earn just to have your kids taken care of. I'm surprised there are not some really big problems around here. It might serve them right if there were. Maybe then they would wise up and deal with the situation.

I have a young daughter who's been married about a year. She and her husband are working and going to school and it's really tough for them. They are having problems making ends meet even without kids. The difference between them and you is that if they really get jammed up, they know they can count on me to help them, but you don't have anybody to turn to. I'd like to think you can count on me in this case. I will certainly play straight with you. I know you didn't take money from all of those wallets. Sure you took money from some of them because you don't have anybody to turn to, but you are not a kleptomaniac who steals everything that's not nailed down. In some cases when things got really desperate, you felt like you had no choice and took some money that did not belong to you, but that's all. And it's not like you were taking it for yourself so you could go out and live it up. You have kids that need things, things that cost money. You didn't take money from all of those wallets, did you? You took some money only from those five on the front row. You did only take the money from those few on the front row, right?

The suspect said nothing—she merely nodded her head in the affirmative. This did not matter to Kenney because he had what he needed, the initial admission. He now had only to get the suspect to fill in the details, a simple task compared to the feat he had just achieved:

I'm glad you told me that because by doing so, you have restored my faith in my ability to measure people. I was beginning to wonder if I had misjudged you. I was beginning to think maybe you really had done all of those things. Now that we have gotten that behind us, let's clear up the details and get on with our lives. I need to know exactly what you did so I can be certain you don't get blamed for other . . .

After she provided the details, signed a statement, and departed, Kenney provided the results to the academy. They dismissed the employee and regarded the incident as closed. The thought of seeking prosecution never seriously crossed anyone's mind because much of what Kenney had told her had at least some element of truth to it.

Analysis

Despite the simplistic nature of this case, the achievement by the interrogator was anything but simple. In the brief encounter with the suspect, Kenney used many techniques to produce the confession. Casual observers might dismiss his efforts as nothing more than the duping of a frightened, poorly educated young woman. Nothing could be further from the truth. He had performed remarkably well and had accomplished what few others could have done.

Few would have thought to bring the picture of the slain officers to the room. Only the accomplished craftsman would have done so. To have placed it where he could casually direct her attention to it would have been done only by a true artist. Without this photograph, nothing that followed would likely have mattered. Flawlessly delivered sales pitches are worthless if nobody hears them. Only the photograph gave the suspect a reason to listen.

Kenney used minimization as his primary pitch. It was a logical choice because by today's standards, it was not much of a crime. The suspect's lack of sophistication regarding the judicial process probably precluded her from understanding this, and she may have thought the location made it more serious in the eyes of the law. Kenney took the time to verbalize the insignificance of the deed. Many investigators would have assumed that the suspect already knew this. Such assumptions contribute to many failures that investigators never understand. What is perfectly obvious to an investigator may be beyond the suspect's understanding. Projection also played a role in painting an acceptable picture of what the suspect had done. Obviously, if the academy had paid her a decent salary, she could have avoided the desperate circumstances that caused her to do what she did. Furthermore, if the academy had shown the caring attitude of many other employers, she would have had a place to take care of her kids while she was working. The academy instead left her to her own devices—what else should they expect?

Did Kenney suggest that she was a drunkard who stole the money to satisfy her craving for alcohol? Absolutely not! She took the money she needed to provide bare necessities for her children. This motive offers no legal defense, but it does make confession more palatable. Although she committed the deed, she did it for a good reason.

Not only did he use all three basic theme tenets, he also used a classic sales principle, gratitude. He let her know he had refused to accept the wholesale indictment of her that many at the academy were making. He had stood up for her and would continue to do so. As a result, she felt indebted to him and needed to respond in kind.

It is difficult to say exactly what produced the confession. The fact remains that Kenney obtained the truth, something few others could have done.

A manual for punctuation and grammar can provide a person with answers to nearly all questions related to those disciplines, but a book about the art of creative writing can only furnish the reader with guidelines and examples. A book dealing with interrogation has the same limitations. Although it can set forth the technical parts of the interrogation process, the art aspects defy description. Diane Sawyer, a newscaster and journalist, when commenting about interviewing, suggested that one can learn to do a journeyman's job in interviewing, and that practice and training can enhance this skill. What she doubted could ever be taught is the aspect of interviewing that is art rather than craft. She summarized by saying that the craftsman will obtain the information sought, but the artist will obtain information that surprises both him or herself and the person being interviewed.

> **Ask your suspects why they confessed— the answer may surprise you.**

While interviewing may be viewed primarily as a craft with a bit of art thrown in, much of interrogation must be considered an art with a bit of magic added on occasion. However, a casual observer might conclude otherwise because the process does not look very impressive. The artistry results from sensing what techniques to use and when to use them. Experienced interrogators have an enormous number of variables open to them. Selecting the proper ones and employing them in precisely the right fashion borders on magic.

If a magician reveals the secret of his or her magic, this revelation will disillusion the recipient of that information because there is no actual magic, just a trick that anyone can duplicate with practice. Casual observers of an interrogation may reach a similar conclusion because nothing they see or hear seems beyond their abilities.

Magicians and interrogators differ in that the former demonstrate a trick after practicing it repeatedly, always doing it the same way until perfected. However, interrogators face a unique set of circumstances every time they confront a suspect. The ability to select the proper techniques and deliver them in just the right way in this arena of infinite possibilities distinguishes the artist from the craftsman. Only investigators who have a genuine interest in people and combine this interest with a willingness to work hard achieve artist status.

Summary

Although some crimes may seem petty and routine to those in law enforcement, in the minds of detained suspects, those same crimes seem monumental. Therefore, good interrogators do not limit their efforts to major crimes, but instead apply the same principles and techniques to each case. By first taking into account a suspect's resistant mindset and the causes of it, the interrogator, seeking to solve a series of petty thefts, was able to overcome that resistance. This enabled him to then effectively present multiple sales pitches, use meaningful props, and apply several sales ploys that ultimately resulted in a confession.

Suggested Reading

Simon, David (1991). *Homicide*. Boston, MA: Houghton Mifflin Company.

Final Thoughts

Technological and scientific advances, publicized by the news media and show business, have caused much of the public and many in law enforcement to believe that remarkable forensic techniques are the means of solving most crimes. However, scientists more often use forensic evidence to confirm guilt than to uncover it. Although important, these advances do not enable investigators to solve most crimes.

People commit crimes, and the solutions to most crimes rest with people as well. Through effective interviewing of both witnesses and victims, investigators are often able to identify the guilty person. Interviewing solves more crimes than any other technique, scientific or otherwise. Often, only after investigators identify the guilty person can scientists use their techniques to confirm the investigators' findings. Even then, many limitations exist that may preclude them from proving the suspect's guilt beyond a reasonable doubt.

Lacking convincing physical evidence or irrefutable witnesses, investigators have no alternative but to try to elicit confessions from the criminals themselves. If they fail, the guilty may go unpunished. Convincing criminals to provide information that will put themselves in jail represents the ultimate investigative coup, and few investigators come to the profession possessing the ability to do this consistently—true artists have always been scarce.

Hopes and prayers not withstanding, we have no reason to believe that this will change with the next generation of police recruits—the Joe Kenneys will always make up only a small part of the law enforcement community. What they know must be collected, systematized, and disseminated to their successors in a comprehensive training program. We must refute the myths that surround interviewing and interrogation, build on the past, and send each new generation into the fray better trained than its predecessors.

As Diane Sawyer suggested: Training may not create many true artists, but it can significantly increase the number of skilled craftsmen.

Index